Teacher's Guide

Finnigin
and Friends
intermediate

Maurice Poe and Barbara A. Schmidt
California State University, Sacramento

Illustrated by Judith A. Moffatt

CURRICULUM ASSOCIATES, INC.
5 Esquire Road, North Billerica MA 01862-2589

Permissions

Curriculum Associates wishes to thank the following authors and publishers for their permission to reprint copyrighted materials.

Page 33:   Poem "Whale" from *Yellow Butter Purple Jelly Red Jam Black Bread* by Mary Ann Hoberman. Copyright 1981 by Mary Ann Hoberman. Reprinted by permission of Viking Penguin, Inc.

Page 37:   Poem "What Night Would It Be?" from *You Read to Me, I'll Read to You* by John Ciardi, (J.B. Lippincott Company). Copyright 1962 by John Ciardi. Reprinted by permission of Harper and Row, Publishers, Inc.

Page 43:   Poem "Pirate Don Durk of Dowdee" by Mildred Meigs from *Faber Book of Nursery Verse,* (Faber and Faber Limited, Publishers).

Page 57:   Song "On Top of Spaghetti" by Tom Glazer. Copyright by Songs Music, Inc., publisher, Scarborough, NY 10510. By permission.

Page 84:   Poem "Sir Smasham Uppe" from *The Flattered Flying Fish and other poems* by E.V. Rieu. Copyright 1962. Reprinted by permission of Methuen and Company.

Page 89:   Poem "I'm So Mad I Could Scream!" from *I'm Mad at You!* by William Cole. Copyright 1978 by William Cole. Reprinted by permission of the author.

Page 94:   Poem "The Triantiwontigongolope" by C.J. Dennis from his *A Book for Kids.* Copyright 1921 by Angus and Robertson Publishers. Reprinted with the permission of Angus and Robertson Publishers.

Page 98:   Poem "Godfrey Gordon Gustavus Gore" by William Brighty Rands from *Home Book of Verse for Young Folks,* (Holt, Rinehart and Winston, Publisher).

Page 131:   Poem "I Found a Four-Leaf Clover" from *The New Kid on the Block* by Jack Prelutsky. Copyright 1984 by Jack Prelutsky. By permission of Greenwillow Books (a division of William Morrow and Company).

Page 136:   American Folk Rhyme "Foolish Questions" adapted by William Cole from *Oh, Such Foolishness!,* poems selected by William Cole. Text copyright by William Cole. Reprinted by permission of Harper and Row, Publishers, Inc.

ISBN 0-89187-529-8
© 1987—Curriculum Associates, Inc.
North Billerica, MA 01862-2589

15 14 13 12 11 10 9 8 7 6 5 4 3 2

Table of Contents

Acknowledgments

Teachers and students in classrooms around the United States helped in determining the rhymes — some old, some new — that give **Finnigin** its wide appeal.

Field-Test Coordinators

Fred Bailey
Principal
Oak Park Elementary School
Bartlesville, Oklahoma

Donald W. Barnickle
Principal
Elmwood Elementary School
Naperville, Illinois

Robert A. Belk
Principal
University Hills School
Rochester, Michigan

Barbara Cockerham
Categorical Program Specialist
Magnolia Elementary School
Riverside, California

Bettye Dean
Reading Specialist
LeGette Elementary School
Fair Oaks, California

Bill Dunlap
Principal
Madison Middle School
Bartlesville, Oklahoma

Robert F. Hillenbrand
Principal
Scott Elementary School
Naperville, Illinois

Lenore Johnson
Principal
Prairie Elementary School
Naperville, Illinois

Mary Anne Kiser
Principal
Maplebrook School
Naperville, Illinois

Leo LaMontagne
Principal
Hunnewell School
Wellesley, Massachusetts

Stephen C. Ligman
Principal
Naper School
Naperville, Illinois

Charles R. Loyd
Assistant Principal
Houser Intermediate School
Conroe, Texas

Jerry Maynard
Principal
Mustang Elementary School
Mustang, Oklahoma

John K. Mealley
Principal
Anna Kyle Elementary School
Fairfield, California

Ruth Michon
Principal
Trajan Demonstration School
Orangevale, California

W. Christine Rauscher
Assistant Superintendent for Curriculum Services
Naperville School District 203
Naperville, Illinois

Jan Rodriguez
Principal
Steeple Run Elementary School
Naperville, Illinois

David N. Rosenquist
Principal
Magnolia Intermediate School
Grass Valley, California

Alice Wells
Principal
Justine Spitalny Elementary School
Phoenix, Arizona

Field-Test Participants

ARIZONA

Phoenix
Justine Spitalny Elementary School
Jane Harmon
Emily Samaniego
Marge Scanlon
Sunland School
Paula M. Maniszko

CALIFORNIA

Fair Oaks
LeGette Elementary School
Clara Beasley
Rosemarie Pantages
Cameron Wilson

Fairfield
Anna Kyle Elementary School
Elizabeth A. Irwin
Kathy Raina

Grass Valley
Magnolia Intermediate School
Sally Johns
Linda Riebe

Orangevale
Trajan Demonstration School
Ralphene Lee

ILLINOIS

Naperville
Ellsworth School
Kim Baker
Elmwood Elementary School
Ginger Fry
Jeffrey Hogan
Maplebrook School
Elise A. Crowell
Steven Denemark
R. Thomas Dewing
Sharon A. Johnson
Naper School
Laura Sullivan
Prairie Elementary School
Sarah Anderson
Marcia Bean
Ann Brotherly
Wendy Cichorz

Scott Elementary School
Ed Dlabal
Debra Meeks
Steeple Run Elementary School
Debra R. Ask
Anna Falk
Jim Gardner

MASSACHUSETTS

North Easton
Easton Middle School
Priscilla A. Olson

Wellesley
Hunnewell School
Sylvia A. Dickey
Nancy B. Lane
Cynthia L. Lawrence

MICHIGAN

Rochester
University Hills School
Diane DeGrande

OKLAHOMA

Bartlesville
Madison Middle School
Sharon Gibson
Oak Park Elementary School
Barbara Rigdon

Mustang
Mustang Elementary School
Elbert R. Vaughan

TEXAS

Conroe
Houser Intermediate School
Mary Evans
Rebecca Keyes

WASHINGTON

Orting
Orting Elementary School
Nora Jangard
Karen Kraucunas
Steven R. Weller

Product Development Department

Susan B. Sizer
Project Manager

Paula F. Beaulieu
Project Editor

Production Department

Kathy J. L. Campbell
Designer

Susan J. Hawk
Graphic Artist

Introduction

Introducing Finnigin and Friends, Intermediate

Need a good laugh? Need a good grin?
Open your door and let Finnigin in!

Laughter and language are remarkable human talents that seem to go together naturally. That's why **Finnigin and Friends** is called the *Good Time with Language* program. It is a supplemental language arts program designed for students in grades 4-6. **Finnigin** blends tongue-tickling, toe-tapping rhymes of universal appeal with language-building experiences that will provide smiles and success for you and your students. Although rhythmic read-aloud and chant-along poems form the core of each lesson, **Finnigin** is a serious language-literacy program. The teacher's guide offers carefully sequenced suggestions for using predictable patterns of language to form a natural bridge between oral and written language. The activities that emerge from each captivating rhyme will actively involve your students in speaking, listening, reading, and writing. With **Finnigin**, language development becomes meaningful, pleasurable, and attainable for *all* students.

Getting to Know
Finnigin and Friends, Intermediate

Finnigin suggests that rhyme, rhythm, and repetition are three important R's for language development. Because the poetry in the program uses familiar language, themes, and concepts, your students will identify with the characters and their antics. Each poem offers opportunities for sharing and relating personal experiences to the characters and situations. **Finnigin's** uniqueness lies in using the poem in each lesson as a catalyst for reproducing, discussing, and extending sounds, words, and ideas.

Finnigin is a flexible program that is enhanced by the fact that the lessons can be used in any order. **Finnigin** is further enhanced by the fact that each lesson can be modified to fit your needs and the needs of your students. It can be used at "teachable moments" or during more structured periods of time.

Finnigin introduces each humorous poem with a purposeful listening activity, followed by choral reading. Choral reading offers a spirited invitation to your students to chime in and chant along, boosting skill and confidence. Shaky readers can be bold, make guesses when they are not sure of words and suffer little risk of failure. With each repeated reading, students reinforce their understanding of sounds, patterns, words, and ideas. Since **Finnigin's** content is appealing, students will enjoy *many* experiences with the text. It is a pleasurable and effective way to practice reading aloud. Most important, your students will feel success as part of a language-using community.

Each poem in **Finnigin** suggests that the teacher first model the oral reading several times. By demonstrating the rhythm, mood, and voice modulation, you set the stage for a variety of chanting experiences. **Finnigin** promotes a teacher-student partnership by sharing fun with language.

Research has demonstrated that the use of predictable materials encourages the development of key language abilities. By design, **Finnigin's** rhymes encourage students to anticipate which word, sentence, or event happens next. The content and activities in **Finnigin** provide learners with experiences to extend language and thinking, and the predictable patterns in **Finnigin** offer opportunities to engage students in valuable writing activities.

Because the language abilities of your students will improve when they are personally and actively involved, **Finnigin** offers specific guidance in effective instructional strategies. You will find many opportunities to create lists of associated ideas for a theme or concept, to probe thinking by modeling questions beyond a literal level, to engage students in partnership and small-group learning, to visualize and identify with the characters and situations in each poem, and to share ideas through dramatizations, art, and written expression.

Finnigin offers multiple opportunities for students to apply thought and language in all content areas. It broadens the students' knowledge by encouraging students to do research on topics related to the themes of the poems. Mastery and control of language will be strengthened as students choose to engage in the many useful activities.

Using the Teacher's Guide

Finnigin has been designed with you and *all* your students in mind. Each lesson offers a step-by-step plan with teacher scripts printed in easy-to-read boldfaced print. Of course, you will want to adapt the script to meet your needs and the needs of your students. Materials needed for each activity are identified throughout the lessons. Because both the teacher's guide and student book contain multiple language activities, you may choose to select those experiences that most appropriately match the learners in your class. Each lesson in the teacher's guide is organized as follows:

1. **Objectives** are listed for each lesson. Activities within each section of the lesson implement these objectives.

2. **Warming Up for Reading** provides specific steps for motivating, focusing attention, and engaging in discussion to identify key concepts and to link prior knowledge to themes.

3. **Sharing the Poem** provides specific steps for guiding choral reading and developing and extending comprehension through oral discussion and dramatization.

4. **Putting Ideas to Work** outlines step-by-step procedures for guiding students through a discussion of the questions listed under "Things to Talk About" in the student book. This section also provides suggestions for assisting students in carrying out activities listed under "Things to Do" in the student book.

5. **Extending Language and Thinking** provides additional activities to extend and develop comprehension and language skills through oral and written language, art, and drama activities.

6. **Strengthening Language for Second-Language Learners** supplies the teacher with a variety of language activities to assist second-language learners in refining oral language skills and relating oral language to print. The activities within this section are valuable for use with all students, not just those learning a second language.

7. **Reaching Across the Curriculum** gives the teacher a variety of multidisciplinary ideas with which to enrich and extend the learner's understanding of language, concepts, and ideas in subject areas commonly taught in the intermediate curriculum.

Using the Student Book

The student book is composed of 32 rhythmic poems. Each poem is introduced by a sentence or question which captures the student's attention and gets the student thinking about the theme of the poem. Each poem is imaginatively illustrated. The illustrations are designed to reinforce the themes and actions of the poems. A section called "Things to Talk About" follows each poem. It is composed of questions that serve as a stimulus for individual, small-group, or whole-class discussion. "Things to Do" is the final section. It provides language-thinking activities related to the themes of the poems. You and your students may select one or all of these activities to do with the whole class or independently.

Launching the Program

Finnigin is for the kid in all of us! It will take you back to your own childhood when rhyme tripped off your tongue and tickled your funny bone. **Finnigin** will take you forward as you delight in your students' achievement and success. What **Finnigin** will not do is stand still! So get ready — let go — and enjoy!

Lesson 1

Michael Finnigin

[handwritten: This is a scripted and very enjoyable lesson. Just follow and say the part in bold writing]

Poor old Michael Finnigin must walk around with a dark cloud hanging over his head! What else could account for his constently bad luck? Your students will identify with this unlucky character ... and discussing the rhythmic language of this well known poem.

[handwritten note: 8:40 Lesson. Follow script — Say the bold + follow directions in between]

Objectives:

Students will
- identify elements of sequence.
- participate in choral/oral reading.
- distinguish between fact and fantasy.
- identify and create cause and effect situations.
- extend language and ideas through oral and written expression.

Warming Up for Reading

Materials
- Chalkboard and chalk

On the chalkboard, write *Grinnigin with Finnigin.*

Today we're going to read about a character who has a lot of problems. The author of this poem had fun making up words to rhyme with the character's name, Finnigin. Let's see how the author did this.

Look at the words I've written on the chalkboard. What are the rhyming words? *(Grinnigin, Finnigin)* **How did the author get** *grin* **to rhyme with** *Finnigin?* *(added -nigin)*

That's right, by adding n-i-g-i-n. What would we have if we added n-i-g-i-n to *begin?* *(beginnigin)* **How about** *chin?* *(chinnigin)* *Skin?* *(skinnigin)* **Good! Now we know how the author made up the words for this poem.**

As I read the poem, listen for the rhyming words. As you listen, see if you can figure out some of Michael Finnigin's problems.

Sharing

Material
- Page 4 in ...

Read the poem expressively emphasizing "beginnigin" at the end of each stanza.

Michael Finnigin

There once was a man named Michael Finnigin.
He grew whiskers on his chinnigin.
The wind came out and blew them innigin,
Poor old Michael Finnigin (beginnigin).

There once was a man named Michael Finnigin.
He went fishing with a pinnigin,
Caught a fish but dropped it innigin,
Poor old Michael Finnigin (beginnigin).

There once was a man named Michael Finnigin,
Climbed a tree and barked his shinnigin,
Took off several yards of skinnigin,
Poor old Michael Finnigin (beginnigin).

There once was a man named Michael Finnigin.
He grew fat and he grew thinnigin,
Had bad luck and couldn't winnigin,
Poor old Michael Finnigin (beginnigin).

Anonymous

Michael Finnigin certainly doesn't lead a dull life, does he? Can you recall the first thing that happened to him? What happened next? What did he use for a hook? Then, what happened? How would you feel if this happened to you?

What happened when he climbed a tree? What do you think the expression "barked his shinnigin" means? What other meanings can you think of for "barked"? What were some other problems Michael Finnigin had that are described in the poem?

I like this tongue-tickler so much that I'm going to read it againnigin! This time join me in saying the last line of each stanza. Read the poem a second time encouraging the students to join in on "Poor old Michael Finnigin (beginnigin)."

Pass out the poem

~~Turn to page 4 in your book.~~ Look at the picture of Michael Finnigin. What is he doing? How does he look? Let's read this poem together. When we come to the "beginnigin" at the end of each stanza, raise your voices to make this word stand out. Don't stop after reading the last stanza! We'll continue until we've read the poem nonstop *two* times. Lead the students in chanting the poem two times without stopping.

This selection lends itself to "Chanting-in-the-Round." Begin by dividing the class into two groups. One group begins reading. When this group reads "chinnigin" at the end of the second line, the second group starts reading. The two groups continue reading until you say, "Stop." On subsequent "Chanting-in-the-Round" readings, the class can be divided into three or four groups. Each group can have its own "Michael Finnigin" to pantomime the action as the group chants its part aloud.

Putting Ideas to Work

Things to Talk About

Material
- ~~Page 5 in student book~~
  Back of page

Look at ~~page 5 in your book~~. "Things to Talk About" asks us to do some thinking about the things that happened to Michael Finnigin.

Read the first set of questions with me. "What is the worst thing that happened to Michael Finnigin? Why?" A lot of bad things happened to Michael Finnigin. Which do you think was the worst? Why?

Some possible student responses
a. His whiskers blew in. That would probably hurt.
b. He dropped the fish back in the water. He might have been hungry.
c. He barked his shin on a tree. That would hurt.

Read the second set of questions with me. "What is the most *unbelievable* thing that happened to him? Why?"

Some possible student responses
a. His whiskers blew in. Whiskers grow out but don't go back in again.
b. Several yards of skin came off his shin. No one has yards of skin on his shin.
c. He grew fat and he grew thin. A person's weight doesn't usually change like that.

Read the third question with me. "What do you think is the cause of Michael Finnigin's bad luck?" We've already talked about all the strange things that happened to Michael Finnigin. Why do you suppose these strange things happened? Use your imagination!

Some possible student responses
a. A witch put an evil spell on him.
b. He lost his lucky penny.
c. A black cat crossed his path.

Things to Do

Materials
- Page 5 in student book
- Writing paper
- Pencils

Look at the "Things to Do" ~~on page 5 in your book.~~ *on back page* **Ask each student to choose one of the three activities to do, or pick one for the whole class to do.**

Let's read number 1 together. "Fold a piece of paper in half the long way. At the top of one half, write Cause. At the top of the other half, write Effect. Under Cause, list all the things Michael Finnigin did. Under Effect, list the results of what he did. Then, make up a cause and effect of your own to add to the lists." Make sure that your cause list shows the things Michael Finnigin did and that your effect list shows what happened when he did these things. Have the students create cause and effect lists.

Let's read number 2 together. "Write a letter to Michael Finnigin suggesting how he might avoid some of the problems he faces in the poem." Michael Finnigin needs some advice. Write him a letter telling him how he might avoid some of his problems. Have the students write letters of advice to Michael Finnigin.

Let's read number 3 together. "Think of some 'Bad Luck' things that have happened to you. Make a list. Share your 'Bad Luck' list with the class." I'm sure that none of you have grown whiskers that have blown in again, but I bet some other "Bad Luck" things have happened to you. What are they? Have the students create "Bad Luck" lists.

Extending Language and Thinking

Activity

Objective
- to identify "sloppy slurs"

Materials
- Chalkboard and chalk
- Strips of paper
- Markers

This selection lends itself to examining the way words are run together in oral language when speakers get lazy.

Introduce the students to "sloppy slurs" by writing run-on sentences on the chalkboard. Ask the students to tell you what these everyday expressions say. On the chalkboard, write the following, leaving out the words in parentheses.

Howyabin? (How have you been?)
Watchyadoin'? (What are you doing?)
Igottabegoin'. (I've got to be going.)

Ask the students to suggest various expressions that people say in which words are run together or often left out. List their expressions on the chalkboard. Discuss what problems "sloppy slurs" can cause in written language.

Invite each student to make up a "sloppy slur," and have him write it on a strip of paper. The students can trade papers and try to translate each other's "slur" into understandable language.

Strengthening Language for Second-Language Learners

Activity

Objectives
- to provide practice in word meaning
- to strengthen sight-word recognition
- to practice using sight words in sentences

Materials
- Chalkboard and chalk
- Index cards
- Markers

On the chalkboard, write the words *in, chin, pin, skin, shin, begin,* and *thin.* Ask the students to copy each word onto an index card. Have them place the cards faceup on their desks.

Read the following sentences aloud. Have the students say the word that fits in each blank, and have them hold up the corresponding word card.

1. **He grew whiskers on his _____ .**
2. **The wind came out and blew them _____ .**
3. **He went fishing with a _____ .**
4. **He climbed a tree and bumped his _____ .**
5. **He began to bleed when he cut the _____ .**
6. **He grew fat and he grew _____ .**
7. **Don't start until I say, "_____ ."**

Point to one of the words on the chalkboard, and ask a student to pronounce the word and to use it in his own sentence.

Reaching Across the Curriculum

Developing Creative Expression

Activity

Objectives
- to discuss feeling "unlucky"
- to complete a sentence about being "unlucky"

Materials
- Chalkboard and chalk
- Writing paper
- Pencils

Michael Finnigin appears to be an "unlucky" person. Discuss the meaning of "unlucky" with the students. **Have you ever felt unlucky? What's happened to you to make you feel unlucky?**

Write the following incomplete sentence on the chalkboard. Have the students copy it and complete the sentence.

Being unlucky is _____ .

(For example, *Being unlucky is when your mom tells you that you can have another piece of pizza, but you find that your brother has eaten it all.*)

Let the students share their sentences and put them in a class-composed book entitled "Unlucky is _____ ."

Expanding Social Studies

Activity

Objectives
- to discuss what it feels like to be laughed at or teased
- to discuss embarrassing moments
- to write about embarrassing moments

Materials
- Chalkboard and chalk
- Writing paper
- Pencils

The author of this poem made light of the unfortunate things that happened to Michael Finnigin. We tend to read the poem with a smile or even laugh aloud at the problems that befall the character. Does this ever happen in real life to you? Do you laugh at other people who are having · problems? Have you ever had a problem and had someone laugh at you? How did you feel? Have you ever been teased? What were you teased about? How did you feel when you were teased? How does it feel to have someone make fun of you? Lead the class in discussing these questions. Discuss the need for more charitable reactions to people's problems and to their own problems.

On the chalkboard, write the word *embarrassing.* Ask the students what the word *embarrassing* means to them. **Have you ever done something embarrassing? What was it? Were other people around? How did these other people react? How did that make you feel?** Have the students describe their most embarrassing moments in writing. Let them share the stories aloud and compare their embarrassing moments and their feelings.

Lesson 2

M. D. Scruggs

Your students will find a lot to laugh about in the surprise ending to this sports saga. M. D.'s football feats will provide the basis for a lively discussion.

Objectives:

Students will
- practice choral/oral reading.
- dramatize actions.
- make inferences about the characters in the poem.
- debate the pros and cons of a social issue.
- engage in problem solving.
- extend language and ideas through oral and written expression.

Warming Up for Reading

Materials
- Chalkboard and chalk

On the chalkboard, write *M. D. Scruggs*.

Our poem today features a character named M. D. Scruggs. The *M* stands for the person's first name, and the *D* stands for the person's middle name. What do you think the initials *M* and *D* stand for? On the chalkboard, write the students' guesses.

The poem we'll share today is about somebody who goes out for the football team. Does this clue change what you think the initials *M. D.* stand for? On the chalkboard, write any additional guesses the students suggest.

This *M. D.* is able to mow down the entire first string of the opposing football team. Do you have any more guesses?

Well, that's enough guessing for now! It's time for you to listen to the poem. You'll find out what the initials *M. D.* really stand for in the surprise ending to the poem.

Sharing the Poem

Materials
- Pages 6-8 in student book

Read the poem dramatically to the students.

M. D. Scruggs

M. D. Scruggs
   came out to practice
   just the other day,
And in a squeaky voice
   announced that,
    "M. D.'s here to play."

The football coach,
   named Jim T. Shurt,
   just frowned and shook his head.
"You're much too small
   to play football
   in minutes you'd be dead."

"I know I'm small.
   I love football.
   I'm tough enough for two.
Give me the ball
   to run one play.
   That's all I ask of you."

"If you insist,
   we'll run a play
   to see what you can do,
But I'm afraid
   those linemen there
   will knock you black and blue."

(continued)

Then M. D. Scruggs
    snatched up the ball
    and charged the sneering line.
That little runt
    smashed Harry Glunt
    and wasted Roger Kline.

Two hundred pounds
    of Tommy Towns
    went under with a fake.
While Huey Hulk,
    with all his bulk,
    was flattened like a cake.

Huge Mike Monroe
    and Kevin Coe
    were steamrolled to the ground.
While Crusher Cruz
    and Billy Bruze
    were mashed into a mound.

"Enough! Enough!"
    yelled Coach T. Shurt.
"That's all I need to see.
    You've won a number on our team,
    and that I guarantee!"

Off came the helmet
    with a cheer,
    the squirt jumped in the air,
And from the team,
    there came a gasp
    when they saw all **her** hair.

"He's not a he.
    He is a **she**,"
    yelled the astonished team.
She smiled and swaggered
    as she said,
    "Just called me Mean Doreen!"

        by Maurice Poe

What did the initials *M. D.* stand for? Was this a surprise to you? Why or why not? The team seemed surprised. Why?

How did the coach react when M. D. Scruggs asked to play? Why? How did the coach feel about her ability to play football *after* he saw her play? What did he tell her?

Do you think the boys will accept Doreen on the team? Why or why not?

~~Turn to page 6 in your book.~~ Look at the pictures on pages 6 and 7. How does M. D. look? Would you think she was a good football player by looking at the picture of her on page 6? What do you think of her when you look at the picture on page 7? Now, look at the picture of M. D. on page 8. Why do you think she is so happy?

Let's read the poem together. When we come to M. D.'s parts, let's read with high voices. When we read the coach's parts, let's try to use deep, gruff voices.

After a few readings by the entire class, divide the class into groups of ~~seven or eight~~ students. Assign one student in each group to be M. D., one to be Coach, ~~three or four~~ to be the team, and two to be narrators; divide the rest of the poem between them. After the groups have had opportunities to practice, invite each group to present the poem to the class. Have the narrators face the class and each character stand with her back to the audience until it's time to read her lines.

1- Narrator
2- Narrator
3. M. D.
4. Coach
5. football team (2 kids if you have extra kids)

Putting Ideas to Work

Things to Talk About

Material
- Page 9 in student book

Look at page 9 in your book. "Things to Talk About" asks us to do some thinking about M. D. Scruggs.

Read the first question with me. "What makes the ending of this poem so surprising?"

Possible student response — M. D. is a girl, not a boy.

Read the second question with me. "How do you think the girl in this poem got the name 'Mean Doreen'?" The poem doesn't tell us how Mean Doreen got her nickname, so we must guess.

Some possible student responses
a. Her friends call her that because she's always been tough.
b. She made up the name for herself after playing a neighborhood football game.
c. Her little brother started calling her that a long time ago.

Read the third question with me. "How do you think Doreen got to be such a good football player?"

Some possible student responses
a. She has brothers who taught her.
b. She watches a lot of football on television and imitates the players.
c. She's just lucky.

Read the fourth question with me. "Why do you think a girl should or shouldn't be allowed to play football?" Do you think Mean Doreen, or any other girl, should be allowed to play football? Why or why not?

Some possible student responses
a. A girl should be allowed to play if she is good at it and wants to play.
b. A girl shouldn't be allowed to play because she might get hurt easily.

Things to Do

Materials
- Page 9 in student book
- Writing paper
- Pencils
- Chalkboard and chalk

Look at the "Things to Do" on page 9 in your book. Ask each student to choose one of the four activities to do, or pick one for the whole class to do.

Let's read number 1 together. "Pretend you are the coach, and you allowed a girl to play on the team. List the problems this might create." On a piece of paper, have each student list problems that might be created by having a girl on the team.

Let's read number 2 together. "Get five or six members of your class together. Divide the poem into reading parts and practice reading aloud. Present the poem to another class." Assign someone to be the narrator, someone to be M. D., and someone to be Coach. Let the rest of the group members be the team. Have them practice until they're ready to perform for another class.

Let's read number 3 together. "Make up a name for a school football team. Write or tell a story about how M. D. Scruggs wins the championship in the final seconds of the game." From the sound of this poem, M. D. Scruggs would be the player to take her team to victory in a championship game. **Write an exciting description of M. D.'s game-winning play.** Have the students write or tell a story about the championship game.

Let's read number 4 together. "Use the
initials of your first and middle names
with your last name to make up a name
that describes the kind of football player
you might be." For example, Edward
William White becomes E. W. White,
otherwise known as Exploding William
White. Terri Ann Poole becomes T. A.
Poole, the one-and-only Tough Ann Poole.
On the chalkboard, write your first and middle
initial and your last name. Ask the students to
think of names that your initials could stand
for. Then, tell each student to use her initials
and last name to make up a good football
nickname. Write each student's *"new"* name on
the chalkboard.

Extending Language and Thinking

Activity

Objectives
- to foster understanding of team sports
- to compare team sports

Materials
- Chalkboard and chalk
- Writing paper
- Pencils
- Encyclopedias
- Chart paper
- Bulletin board
- Marker
- Newspaper articles and photographs
- Tacks

Ask the students to tell you the most popular
team sports played at school. Write the names of
these sports across the top of the chalkboard.
On the left side of the chalkboard, list the
following: *Points per Score, Time of Year,
Contact/Non-Contact, Male/Female, Number of
Players, Equipment,* and *Kind of Uniform.* Use
the following sample as a guide:

	Football	Baseball	Basketball	Soccer
Points per Score				
Time of Year				
Contact/Non-Contact				
Male/Female				
Number of Players				
Equipment				
Kind of Uniform				

Divide the class into groups. Have each group
copy the chart from the chalkboard and fill in
the information. Then, have the groups compare
their completed charts. Let the students use
encyclopedias to resolve any disagreements over
information.

Make a large chart summarizing the information
generated by the students. Post the chart on a
bulletin board entitled "Our Favorite Sports."
Encourage the students to bring in newspaper
articles and photographs of their favorite teams
and players. Place these articles and photographs around the chart.

Strengthening Language for Second-Language Learners

Activity

Objective
- to discuss favorite sports

Material
- None

Ask the students to identify their favorite sports.
Lead a class discussion about why the students
like these sports and what abilities a person
needs to do well in these sports. Encourage the
students to bring in pictures of their favorite
teams and players.

Reaching Across the Curriculum

Expanding Social Studies

Activity 1

Objective
- to debate the issue of girls playing football

Materials
- Chalkboard and chalk

This selection is a natural lead-in to a discussion about the role of women in sports. On the chalkboard, write *Should girls play football?* Moderate a class debate in which one group of four or five students takes the "pro" position, and another group of four or five students takes the "con" position. Instruct the debating students to think of reasons why girls should or should not play football. Each team should present its argument to the rest of the class. Then, ask the audience to suggest additional points that were not brought up by the two teams. You may also want to have the students vote to determine which side they felt presented the most convincing argument.

Activity 2

Objective
- to research successful women athletes

Materials
- Library sources

Suggest that interested students do some research on successful women athletes. Have the students share the information they find with the rest of the class.

Developing Creative Expression

Activity

Objective
- to produce a sports newscast

Materials
- Radio or television
- Newspapers
- Chalkboard and chalk

Have the students work in groups to produce a sports newscast. Let the students listen to radio and television sports reports. Have them read the newspaper for information for their own newscast.

Tell the students that there should be three parts to their newscasts. One part of each program should cover local sporting events, and a second part should cover national events. A third part should be an interview with M. D. Scruggs, the heroine who helped her team win the championship football game.

On the chalkboard, write the following program outline for the students to use.

Sports in the News
  I. *Opening*
 II. *Local sports (two or three minutes)*
III. *National sports (two or three minutes)*
IV. *Interview with celebrity (two or three minutes)*
  V. *Closing*

What's Your Excuse?

Who could help but identify with the familiar pastime of making up far-fetched excuses? Listen to the students in this imaginative chant who offer implausible but familiar reasons for not completing their homework assignment on time.

Objectives:

Students will
- brainstorm a list of excuses as a prereading activity.
- practice choral/oral reading.
- engage in choral theater.
- extend language and ideas through oral and written expression.

Warming Up for Reading

Material
- None

Has there ever been a time when you came up with an excuse for not doing something you were supposed to do? I can remember an excuse I came up with once when I was your age. Share a personal experience with your students, and ask them to offer excuses that they have used.

From the sound of your experiences, you will have a lot of *empathy* with the students in the poem you are about to hear. *Empathy* is a new word for us. What do you think it means? Encourage the students' responses before clarifying that *empathy* means "sharing another's feelings and ideas."

Sharing the Poem

Materials
- Pages 10-11 in student book

Read the poem expressively to the students.

What's Your Excuse?

"Where is *your* homework?"
Asked Mrs. Longday.
"I'm sure that *you* knew
It was due by today!"

The first one to answer
Was Sally McFall
Who told how her small dog
Had eaten it all.

Then Shelly Kay Kisser
Said, heaving a sigh,
"I don't have my homework
And I don't know why."

"Where is *your* homework?"
Asked Mrs. Longday.
"I'm sure that *you* knew
It was due by today!"

The next one to answer
Was Billy Joe Slatt
Who said that his homework
Was chewed by a rat.

"And mine disappeared
Right into thin air,"
Said a frowning young lady
Named Maggie Lou Clare.

"Where is *your* homework?"
Asked Mrs. Longday.
"I'm sure that *you* knew
It was due by today!"

"It was awful!" said Raymond.
"I cannot explain
How my homework just vanished.
It went down the drain."

(continued)

> "A gorilla took mine
> And wouldn't give it back,"
> Whispered a student
> named Jonathan Black.
>
> Mrs. Longday just smiled
> As she nodded her head.
> She waited a moment.
> Then here's what she said.
>
> "The excuses you tell me
> Deserve a big **A.**
> Instead, get to work.
> There's no recess today!"
>
> *by Barbara Schmidt and Maurice Poe*

Which student did you *empathize* with the most? In other words, whose excuse made the most sense to you personally? Which student do you think had the most vivid imagination? Why? What do you think about Mrs. Longday's reaction to the excuses?

Pass out poem

Turn to page 10 in your book. Look at the pictures on pages 10 and 11. What do you see? How do you think the teacher feels about using these animals for excuses? Before we read the poem together, we need some volunteers to take the parts of the teacher and each of the students. We'll also need a narrator to read the other parts. Let's try sharing the poem in a *Reader's Theater* style. Here's how it works. You'll line up in front of the room with your back to the audience. As we come to your part, you'll turn around, face the audience, and read that part. It's easy to know who reads when the quotation marks give you a clue, but what will you do about Sally McFall and Billy Joe Slatt? Involve the students in deciding how to divide the speaking parts. Encourage appropriate facial expressions, gestures, and voice quality. Several practices may precede a final production that can be shared with other classes.

Follow along as we read

Quotation marks

Reader's Theater

Putting Ideas to Work

Things to Talk About

Material
- Page 12 in student book

Look at page 12 in your book. "Things to Talk About" asks us to do some thinking about excuses.

Read number 1 with me. "What else could Mrs. Longday have said or done to her students?" Mrs. Longday punished her students by not allowing them to go to recess. What else could she have said or done?

Some possible student responses
a. She could have given each student an "F" for the homework assignment.
b. She could have given the class twice as much homework for the next day.
c. She could have written letters to the students' parents, telling them to make sure their children complete their homework assignments.

Read number 2 with me. "Who do you think came up with the best excuse?"

Some possible student responses — Sally McFall, Maggie Lou Clare, Jonathan Black

Read number 3 with me. "What is the best excuse you ever gave?" Being a teacher, I've heard a lot of good excuses from students like you. I want to hear the best excuse you've ever used. Have the students tell the best excuses they've ever used.

Some possible student responses
a. My little brother ate my homework.
b. My house was flooded, and my homework floated away.
c. We lost our electricity last night, and I couldn't see to do my homework.

Read number 4 with me. "Tell about a time when an excuse got you into trouble." Some people wouldn't be as understanding as Mrs. Longday, especially after hearing such crazy and unbelievable excuses. Tell about a time when you used an excuse and

got into trouble. Have the students tell about times when excuses got them into trouble.

Some possible student responses
a. I told my mother I didn't empty the trash because I got home so late, but my little sister told my mother I was home early.
b. I told my teacher I was late for school because we got stuck in traffic, but she found out I had overslept.

Things to Do

Materials
- Page 12 in student book
- Writing paper
- Pencils

Look at the "Things to Do" on page 12 in your book. Ask each student to choose one of the activities to do, or pick one for the whole class to do.

Let's read number 1 together. "Think of a task that is your responsibility, like babysitting, doing your share of the housework, or managing your allowance. Write down four excuses for not fulfilling your responsibility. Decide whether each excuse is reasonable and makes sense or unreasonable and might get you into trouble. Next to each excuse, write *reasonable* or *unreasonable*." Have the students generate lists of excuses. Then, lead a class discussion based on these lists.

Let's read number 2 together. "Use the following story starter to write a story. The funniest thing happened to make me late for school today. I was _____ ." Write a paragraph that begins with this idea. Use your imagination! Have the students write paragraphs about why they were late for school.

Extending Language and Thinking

Activity 1

Objective
- to write a paragraph on excuses

Materials
- Chalkboard and chalk
- Writing paper
- Pencils

You all had such empathy for those poor students who didn't have their homework done. Let's think about another situation when we were tempted to come up with excuses for not accomplishing something we were supposed to do. I'll put that situation in the middle of a circle on the chalkboard.

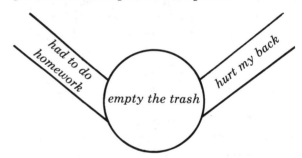

Now, I'm going to put some spokes coming out of the circle. Help me think of some good excuses to put on the spokes.

Now, it's your turn. With a partner, think up a task to put in your circle, and then put at least four excuses on spokes around the circle. Have each student work with his partner to list tasks and excuses. Let the students share their lists with the whole class.

Now, you're ready to take your good ideas and develop a juicy paragraph on excuses. How could you start your paragraph? Then, how will you write about your excuses? What will you say at the end of your paragraph? Help the students organize a sequence of sentences. Paragraphs can be shared, edited, revised, and displayed as final drafts.

Activity 2

Objective
- to write different versions of the poem

Materials
- Copies of incomplete stanzas from the poem
- Pencils

Distribute copies of individual stanzas from the poem. Leave the last two lines of each stanza blank so that the students can write their own versions. For example:

Then Shelly Kay Kisser
Said, heaving a sigh,
" _____ _____ _____ _____ _____
_____ _____ _____ _____ _____ . "

Another new version of the poem can be written using the names of students in the class.

Strengthening Language for Second-Language Learners

Activity

Objectives
- to promote understanding of ending punctuation marks
- to use ending punctuation marks

Materials
- Chalkboard and chalk
- Index cards
- Marker

This poem offers the opportunity to discuss punctuation marks found at the end of different kinds of sentences. On the chalkboard, write *Where is your homework?* Ask the students what kind of a sentence this is. **What lets us know that this sentence is a question? Can you give other examples of questions?**

On the chalkboard, write *I don't have my homework.* Ask the students what kind of sentence this is. **How does this sentence end? Can you give other examples of telling sentences?**

On the chalkboard, write *It was awful! No recess today!* Ask the students what kind of sentences these are. **How does each sentence end? What other statements can teachers and students make that are filled with excitement?**

Write ending punctuation marks on index cards. Make a set for each student. As you say a sentence, have each student hold up a card showing the appropriate punctuation mark.

Reaching Across the Curriculum

Fostering Good Study Habits

Activity

Objectives
- to discuss good study habits
- to list tips to improve study habits

Materials
- Writing paper
- Pencils

This poem offers an opportunity to involve the students in a discussion of their own study habits. Ask the students to brainstorm responses to the following questions. **What helps you do your homework? What interferes with doing your homework?** Let each student develop his own list of tips to help him get his homework done.

Expanding Social Studies

Activity

Objective
- to discuss the uses and abuses of excuses

Material
- None

The humorous excuses in this poem may give rise to a class discussion on the uses and abuses of excuses. **What is a legitimate excuse? What forces beyond our control contribute to excuses?** Present the students with a problem situation, like being late for school, not bringing lunch money, not returning a library book. After the students suggest possible reasons for these circumstances, lead a class discussion about the validity of the excuses.

Lesson 4

Bocca-Wacca-Wattamus

This funny rhyme tickles the tongue and the funny bone! Students will chuckle over Ryan O'Brien's unique requests.

Objectives:

Students will
- practice choral/oral reading.
- dramatize the action in this poem.
- engage in visualizing images.
- generate vivid descriptions.
- identify personal favorites.
- extend language and ideas through oral and written expression.

Warming Up for Reading

Materials
- Chalkboard and chalk

On the chalkboard, write *Today's Menu — Bocca-Wacca-Wattamus.*

Look what's for lunch today! When was the last time you had bocca-wacca-wattamus for lunch? *What?* You *never* ate bocca-wacca-wattamus? Well, I never heard of it either until I read the poem we share today. The boy in our poem asks for bocca-wacca-wattamus every time he goes to eat in a restaurant. I wonder if the people in the restaurant know what he's talking about. What do you think bocca-wacca-wattamus tastes like? It sure is hard to say. Say it with me. Bocca-Wacca-Wattamus! Now, listen to the poem to see if you can figure out what bocca-wacca-wattamus is.

Sharing the Poem

Materials
- Pages 13-14 in student book
- Simple props for acting out the poem

Read the poem dramatically to the students.

(Turn the page for the poem.)

Bocca-Wacca-Wattamus

They took Ryan O'Brien to breakfast
and asked what he wanted to eat.
His mother looked very nervous
as he wiggled around in his seat.

**"I want bocca-wacca-wattamus and salamander stew,
riggle-raggle ragamuffins, rutabagas, too.
I want diffy-daffy dandelions and then, for my dessert,
a dish of loony lingaberries smothered with fresh dirt."**

"Ryan!" squealed his mother.
"Wow!" said his sister.
"Yuck!" said his brother.
"We're all out," said the waiter.

They took Ryan O'Brien to lunch
at the best restaurant in the town.
His mother looked very nervous
as the family began to sit down.

**"I want bocca-wacca-wattamus and salamander stew,
riggle-raggle ragamuffins, rutabagas, too.
I want diffy-daffy dandelions and then, for my dessert,
a dish of loony lingaberries smothered with fresh dirt."**

"Ryan!" squealed his mother.
"Wow!" said his sister.
"Yuck!" said his brother.
"Not in season," said the waitress.

They took Ryan O'Brien to dinner
"and what will you have today?"
His mother looked very nervous
as Ryan began to say,

**"I want bocca-wacca-wattamus and salamander stew,
riggle-raggle ragamuffins, rutabagas, too.
I want diffy-daffy dandelions and then, for my dessert,
a dish of loony lingaberries smothered with fresh dirt."**

"Ryan!" squealed his mother.
"Wow!" said his sister.
"Yuck!" said his brother.
"Medium or rare?" said the waiter.

by Barbara Schmidt

Did you figure out what bocca-wacca-wattamus is? Do you think there really is such a thing? What about riggle-raggle ragamuffins? I've never heard of those either. There are many strange-sounding foods in this poem! Why do you think Ryan's mother got nervous? Why did his sister say "Wow!"? Why did his brother say "Yuck!"? What do you think the waitress meant when she said, "Not in season"? Do you think Ryan was surprised when the waiter said, "Medium or rare?" Why? Why not? What do you think *your* family would say if you asked for some crazy foods the way Ryan did?

Listen as I read the poem again. Pick out a food that you like the sound of the best. Read the poem several times encouraging the students to chant along on the chorus.

Which food do you like best? Those words are really tongue twisters. Turn to page 13 in your book. Look at the picture. Who do you see in the picture? Can you tell how the people feel by looking at the picture? How can you tell? I need your help with Ryan's part. We're also going to need someone to be the mother, the sister, the brother, the waiters, and the waitress. Now, we're ready to read along in our books. Have the class read the poem chorally several times with individual students taking the parts of the mother, sister, brother, waiters, and waitress. Ryan's part can be chanted by the whole class through several readings until individual students are ready to take the part.

"Bocca-Wacca-Wattamus" is a good story-poem to act out. Why do you think I called it a story-poem? That's right! It does tell a little story about Ryan. It also has some things that stories have. The poem tells us *where* things are happening, *who* is in the story, and *what* happens.

If we are going to act out this poem, we need to know *where* Ryan goes. Can you tell me? We will need three different restaurants. Think of names for the restaurants, so we can make restaurant signs and put them on three desks.

Who is in the story-poem? We'll need name tags on yarn to put around the necks of the people in our story-poem. *What* do these people do, and *what* do they say?

We'll need to practice saying what happens in the poem so that our audience knows what's happening. Have the students make signs, tags, and props. Give them time to practice before performing in front of an audience.

Putting Ideas to Work

Things to Talk About

Material
- Page 15 in student book

Look at page 15 in your book. "Things to Talk About" tells us to do some thinking about Ryan O'Brien.

Read the first set of questions with me. "Does Ryan O'Brien remind you of anyone? Who?" Have the students tell who Ryan O'Brien reminds them of and why.

Read the second question with me. "How would you react to Ryan if you were sitting with him in a restaurant?" Ryan's probably a little different than anyone you've ever gone to a restaurant with before! How do you think you would react to his odd request?

Some possible student responses
a. I'd sink down in my chair in embarrassment.
b. I'd laugh at him.
c. I'd move to another table and pretend I didn't know him.

Read the third question with me. "How would you react to Ryan if you were taking his order in a restaurant?" We just talked about how you would react if you were sitting with Ryan. Now, think about how you would react to Ryan if you were taking his order. What would you do or say?

Some possible student responses
a. I'd ask him to repeat his order to make sure I heard what he was saying correctly.
b. I'd try not to laugh and tell him that he could order only what is on the menu.
c. I'd ask him to describe the foods so I could see if the cook would make a special order for him.

Read the fourth question with me. "Do you think the waiters and waitress really know what Ryan's talking about?"

Some possible student responses
a. Yes, because they respond normally.
b. No, they're just joking when they answer him.

Things to Do

Materials
- Page 15 in student book
- Drawing paper
- Crayons
- Writing paper
- Pencils

Look at the "Things to Do" on page 15 in your book. Ask each student to choose one of the three activities to do, or pick one for the whole class to do.

Let's read number 1 together. "Make a menu for your favorite restaurant. Draw pictures of some of the selections you can order at the restaurant. Write the names of the selections and the prices." Your menu can be for a real or make-believe restaurant. Be sure to include a wide variety of foods. Have the students make illustrated menus.

Let's read number 2 together. "Think up some crazy-sounding foods of your own. Write descriptions of how your foods look, taste, and smell." Have the students write descriptions of imaginary foods.

Let's read number 3 together. "What's *your* favorite food to order when you eat out? Write a mouth-watering description of this food without telling what it is. See if other students can guess what food you are describing." Have the students write descriptions of their favorite foods.

Extending Language and Thinking

Activity

Objectives
- to draw pictures of the foods in the poem
- to describe the foods

Materials
- Drawing paper
- Crayons
- Chalkboard and chalk

Have you ever noticed that some restaurants show pictures of the foods you can order? I've never seen a picture in a restaurant of bocca-wacca-wattamus or riggle-raggle ragamuffins or diffy-daffy dandelions or loony lingaberries. We're going to help the restaurant out by drawing some pictures of these foods. Pass out drawing paper and crayons.

Fold your paper into four squares. Draw a picture of one of Ryan's foods in each square. Help me remember what those foods were. I'll list them on the chalkboard. On the chalkboard, list the four foods mentioned in the preceding paragraph. Have the students draw pictures of the foods.

I'm not sure our pictures will be enough to give somebody an idea of what these foods are like. Help me think of some words that tell about the foods. What do you think bocca-wacca-wattamus *looks* like? Give me some words that tell. What do you think bocca-wacca-wattamus *tastes* like? Give me some tasty words. What do you think bocca-wacca-wattamus *smells* like? Give me some words. On the chalkboard, list the descriptive words about bocca-wacca-wattamus offered by the students. Then, do the same for riggle-raggle ragamuffins, diffy-daffy dandelions, and loony lingaberries.

Strengthening Language for Second-Language Learners

Activity 1

Objective
- to discuss and dramatize restaurant behavior

Material
- None

Have the students act out what happens when they go to a restaurant. Use the following questions to initiate a discussion. **Do you ever go out to eat at restaurants? Where do you go? What do you get to eat? Show us how you act at a restaurant. Can you think of some polite things to say or do at a restaurant?**

Activity 2

Objective
- to identify favorite restaurant foods and favorite at-home foods

Materials
- Drawing paper and crayons
- Marker and chart

Ask each student to draw two pictures, one of her favorite restaurant food and one of her favorite at-home food. Have the student label her foods, and place the pictures in the appropriate columns on a wall chart. Have one column entitled "Eating-Out Favorites" and the other entitled "At-Home Favorites."

Reaching Across the Curriculum

Expanding Social Studies

Activity 1

Objective
- to create restaurant menus

Materials
- Menus from different restaurants
- Construction paper and markers

Have the students collect menus and bring them to class. Discuss what one might expect to find on a menu. Have the students create their own menus, writing the names of their restaurants on the covers. Tell the students to decide what foods to serve and how much the foods will cost.

Activity 2

Objective
- to develop a class cookbook

Materials
- Recipes
- Pencils and duplicating masters

Develop a class ethnic cookbook. Ask the students to bring in recipes from home. Let the students copy the recipes on duplicating masters, and have them draw pictures on the masters to illustrate the recipes.

Activity 3

Objective
- to role play the activities of a waiter and waitress

Material
- None

Have the class role play the activities of waiters and waitresses. Keep in mind that the students' experiences may be quite different from your own. Discuss appropriate behavior for a waiter or waitress. Role play situations that portray positive and negative behavior by a waiter or waitress.

Sharing Literature

Activity

Objectives
- to share a poem
- to discuss the dangers of eating strange foods

Material
- Children's book
  Starbird, Kaye. *Don't Ever Cross a Crocodile.* Philadelphia: J.B. Lippincott Company, 1963.

Share the poem "Eat-It-All Elaine" by Kaye Starbird from *Don't Ever Cross a Crocodile.* This can lead to a discussion on the dangers of eating strange foods.

Ladles and Jelly Spoons

No wonder the audience boos when Fenster Gore gives this mixed-up, muddled announcement of a coming event! Your students will enjoy clapping, booing, and cheering as they listen to and read the poem.

Objectives:

Students will
- understand the concept of "contradictory information."
- practice choral/oral reading.
- identify elements of absurdity in the poem.
- describe qualities of effective speakers.
- extend language and ideas through oral and written expression.

Warming Up for Reading

Materials
- Chalkboard and chalk

On the chalkboard, write *Ladies and Gentlemen.*

You are about to hear the most ridiculous announcement for any meeting that I've ever heard! Instead of beginning the announcement with "Ladies and Gentlemen," the character in this poem says, "Ladles and Jelly Spoons." And if you think that's a silly beginning, keep your ears open for all the other foolish things the character Fenster Gore says.

Sharing the Poem

Materials
- Chalkboard and chalk
- Pages 16-17 in student book

Read the poem aloud with exaggerated expression.

Ladles and Jelly Spoons

Narrator:
Announcements of our meeting
Will be made by Fenster Gore —
Who's known throughout this city
As a windbag and a bore.

Fenster:
Ladles and jelly spoons:
I come here before you
To quietly shout
An important event
I know nothing about.

Next Thursday or Friday,
But don't mark the date,
We're having a meeting.
Be sure and come late.

Admission is free,
But you pay at the door.
I'll save you a front seat,
So sit on the floor.

Chorus:
Clap! Clap!
Hear! Hear!
Stomp! Stomp!
Cheer! Cheer!
Hiss! Hiss!
Boo! Boo!

(continued)

> *Fenster:*
> Dress up in your best clothes,
> Rags dirty and torn.
> Please be very quiet,
> Except for your horn.
>
> They'll have tea and cookies,
> But no one can eat.
> And when they say stand up,
> Just stay in your seat.
>
> Let us know tomorrow,
> If you'll stay home that day.
> And tell us what speech,
> You'll forget how to say.
>
> We thank you for being
> So patient and rude.
> The last time I spoke here
> The audience booed.
>
> ***Chorus:***
> **Clap! Clap!**
> **Hear! Hear!**
> **Stomp! Stomp!**
> **Cheer! Cheer!**
> **Hiss! Hiss!**
> **Boo! Boo!**
>
> *Anonymous*

Fenster Gore sure is weird! He makes so many silly *contradictions* in this poem! What do you think the word *contradictions* means? On the chalkboard, write the word *contradictions* and discuss its meaning.

Now, I'm going to read the poem again. This time do what the chorus suggests, so clap, stomp, cheer, hiss, and boo. Read through the poem a second time encouraging the students to participate in the chorus.

Turn to page 16 in your book. Look at the picture of Fenster Gore. What is he doing? How does he look? Look at the picture of the lady on page 17. See if you can find the ridiculous *contradiction* that goes with that picture.

Now, let's read the poem together. Then, we'll need a volunteer to be the narrator and some brave person to be Fenster Gore. Lead the students in reading the poem chorally. Then, have individual students take the parts of the narrator and Fenster, with the whole class acting out the chorus.

Putting Ideas to Work

Things to Talk About

Materials
- Pages 16-18 in student book

Look at page 18 in your book. "Things to Talk About" asks us to do some thinking about Fenster's crazy speech.

Read the first question with me. "What makes this poem so ridiculous?"

Possible student response — It is full of contradictions.

Read the second question with me. "How many opposite statements does Fenster make in his announcement?" Read through the poem quickly and quietly. See if you can count how many times Fenster contradicts himself. I bet it's a lot.

Possible student response — thirteen times

Read the third question with me. "What advice would you give Fenster before his next speech?" Fenster obviously needs some advice about giving speeches. What would you tell him to help make him a better speaker?

Some possible student responses

a. Get your facts straight.
b. Rehearse your speech a few times so you don't get mixed-up.
c. Call your audience "Ladies and Gentlemen," not "Ladles and Jelly Spoons."

Read the fourth question with me. "How does the audience's reaction affect Fenster?" An audience's reaction can really affect a speaker. When an audience cheers, the speaker feels good. When an audience boos and hisses, the speaker doesn't feel so good. **How do you think** *this* **audience's reaction affects Fenster Gore?** Lead a class discussion about how this audience's reaction must confuse Fenster. The audience claps and cheers, and then hisses and boos.

Things to Do

Materials
- Page 18 in student book
- Writing paper
- Pencils

Look at the "Things to Do" on page 18 in your book. Ask each student to choose one of the three activities to do, or pick one for the whole class to do.

Let's read number 1 together. "How might Fenster Gore announce a camping trip, a birthday party, or a new movie in town? Write your own version of one of these announcements in Fenster Gore style." Have the students write announcements in the contradictory style used by Fenster Gore.

Let's read number 2 together. "Write about a time when you spoke to an audience. What did you say? How did you feel? How did the audience react?" Have the students write about times when they spoke in front of a group.

Let's read number 3 together. "Write a *serious* **announcement for a class meeting. Be sure to list all the necessary information."** Include the time and place of the meeting and, most important, the reason for the meeting. Have the students write meeting announcements.

Extending Language and Thinking

Activity 1

Objectives
- to identify contradictions in the poem
- to create additional contradictions

Materials
- Writing paper
- Pencils

This poem reminds me of "Good News" and "Bad News." It tells us one thing and then twists it around. See if you can identify the "Good News" parts of the poem and the "Bad News" parts. Fold your paper into two columns. Write *Good News* at the top of one column and *Bad News* at the top of the second column. Then, list the "Good News" parts from the poem in one column and the contradictions in the other column.

After you've identified the "Good News" and "Bad News" from the poem, think up some more "Good News" and "Bad News" that could happen at this meeting. Add at least two ideas of your own to the list.

Activity 2

Objective
- to teach awareness of good speaking and listening skills

Materials
- Chart paper
- Marker

What makes an audience "boo" a speaker? What are some things that a speaker should be aware of so that the audience tunes in with appreciation and enjoyment to the message? What are the responsibilities of the listeners? Write the students' responses on a chart entitled "Speak Up!" and "Listen Up!" On the chart, list some of the qualities of effective speaking and listening. Call the students' attention to the chart as they prepare reports, summarize stories, give presentations, etc.

Strengthening Language for Second-Language Learners

Activity

Objective
- to discuss how confusing English can be

Material
- None

Check to see if the students understand the absurdities in this poem. Lead a discussion about how a new language is often confusing. Encourage the students to talk about times when they were bewildered by English. Explain that you have often had similar experiences with your own language. Give examples of these experiences. Discuss how to handle such situations.

Reaching Across the Curriculum

Developing Creative Expression

Activity 1

Objective
- to create a poster announcing a meeting

Materials
- Poster board
- Markers

If you were making a poster announcing a meeting, what important information would need to appear on the poster? Encourage the students to identify the key elements of an announcement. Have them

include the date, time, place, purpose, etc. **Create a poster announcing Fenster Gore's meeting!**

Activity 2

Objective
- to describe qualities of effective speakers and listeners

Material
- None

Have you ever given a talk in front of an audience? Describe your experience. What was the topic of your speech? How did you feel? How did the audience react? What would you do differently next time? What advice would you give to listeners in an audience that would be helpful to the speaker? Lead the class in a discussion about the art of public speaking.

Expanding Social Studies

Activity

Objectives
- to discuss the purposes of meetings
- to locate information about meetings

Materials
- Newspapers
- Writing paper
- Pencils

Fenster Gore's announcement told about an unusual meeting. Have you ever attended a meeting? What kind of meeting was it? What happened at the meeting? Why are meetings held?

Look in the newspaper to find announcements for organizations that hold meetings. Find out what goes on at these meetings. Make a list of purposes for meetings. Help the students locate information in the newspaper about meetings being held around the world. Discuss the purposes of these meetings. On a piece of paper, have the students write down the purposes of these meetings.

Lesson 6

Whale

A whale of a time is in store for your class with Mary Ann Hoberman's humorous ode about the self-image of the world's largest mammal. Self-acceptance is the theme of this rhyme.

Objectives:

Students will

- identify and verify factual information about whales.
- practice choral/oral reading.
- identify descriptive words.
- extend language and ideas through oral and written expression.

Warming Up for Reading

Materials

- Chart paper
- Marker
- Chalkboard and chalk
- Index cards
- Pencils

On chart paper, draw a large outline of a whale.

We've got a whale of a tale today! Did you know that whales are the largest mammals alive in the world today? Can you tell me some other facts about whales?

On the chalkboard, write *Whales* _____ . Divide the class into pairs. Give each pair an index card and a pencil. **You and your partner have five minutes to think of a fact about whales. Write your fact on the index card. Be sure to write your fact in the form of the sentence frame I've written on the chalkboard.**

Once the students have written down their facts about whales, tape the index cards inside the outline of the whale on the chart paper. Discuss the information written on each card.

You've gathered a large *body* of serious information about whales. We'll be using some of your data later. Right now, we're going to hear how poetess Mary Ann Hoberman looks at whales. As you'll soon find out, she doesn't look at whales quite as seriously as we just have! As I read the poem, see if you can figure out the message of the poem.

Sharing the Poem

Material

- Page 19 in student book

Read the poem in a lighthearted manner putting particular emphasis on the last stanza.

Whale

A whale is stout about the middle,
He is stout about the ends,
& so is all his family
& so are all his friends.

He's pleased that he's enormous,
He's happy he weighs tons,
And so are all his daughters
And so are all his sons.

He eats when he is hungry
Each kind of food he wants,
& so do all his uncles
& so do all his aunts.

(continued)

He doesn't mind his blubber,
He doesn't mind his creases,
& neither do his nephews
& neither do his nieces.

You may find him chubby,
You may find him fat,
But he would disagree with you:
He likes himself like that.

by Mary Ann Hoberman

What words describe the way this whale feels about himself? Encourage the students to discuss the whale's confidence and self-satisfaction.

This is a poem about whales, but what does it have to do with humans? Discuss the poem's theme, the importance of self-acceptance.

Turn to page 19 in your book. Look at the picture of the whale. Can you tell how he feels by the way he looks? How do you think he feels? Let's read the poem together. Lead the students in a group reading of the poem.

Putting Ideas to Work

Things to Talk About

Materials
- Page 20 in student book
- Chalkboard and chalk

Look at page 20 in your book. "Things to Talk About" asks us to do some thinking about the whale.

Read the first question with me. "What are some unique physical qualities of the whale in the poem?" Look at the poem and find the words that describe what the whale looks like. What are they? List the students' responses on the chalkboard.

Some possible student responses — stout, enormous, chubby

Read the second question with me. "Which words in the poem describe how the whale feels about himself?" List the students' responses on the chalkboard.

Some possible student responses — pleased, happy, likes himself

Read the third question with me. "Why do you think this whale feels so good about himself?" Even though he's "enormous" and "weighs tons," this whale feels good about himself. Why?

Some possible student responses
a. He's like his family and friends.
b. He's happy inside and likes himself.
c. He feels good about himself because whales are supposed to be big and fat.

Things to Do

Materials
- Page 20 in student book
- Drawing paper
- Crayons
- Writing paper
- Pencils
- Chart paper
- Markers

Look at the "Things to Do" on page 20 in your book. Ask each student to choose one of the three activities to do, or pick one for the whole class to do.

Let's read number 1 together. "Draw a cartoon showing the whale with a self-satisfied expression on his face. Put a 'talking bubble' above his head. Have him say how he feels about his appearance." Have the students draw cartoons about the whale.

Let's read number 2 together. "Select any animal of your choice. Use the pattern of the 'Whale' poem to create your own poem. Describe the appearance of the animal and his family members, and tell how the animal feels about himself." Have the students write poems about animals.

Let's read number 3 together. "Brainstorm a list of words that describe physical qualities of the students in your class. Write your words on a chart." On a chart, have the students write lists of words that describe physical characteristics of their fellow students. At the top of the chart, write "Students in Room _____ ."

Extending Language and Thinking

Activity 1

Objective
- to locate additional facts about whales

Materials
- Whale chart from **Warming Up for Reading**
- Library sources
- Index cards
- Pencils
- Tape

What *facts* did the poem offer about whales? Let's see if there are any new ones that we can add to our whale chart. Encourage the students to use library sources to locate any new information about whales. Have them write their facts on index cards, and tape them to the chart.

Activity 2

Objective
- to recognize and contrast fact and opinion

Materials
- Chalkboard and chalk
- Writing paper
- Pencils

Which statements in the poem are *not* facts, but opinions? How do you know? What's the difference between a fact and an opinion?

On the chalkboard, write *Students in Room* _____ . Under this title, make two columns. At the top of one column, write *Facts* and at the top of the other, write *Opinions*. **Give me a fact about a student in this class.** Encourage the students to give positive rather than negative facts and opinions. Under *Facts,* write the first positive response you receive. **Now, how about an opinion?** Under *Opinions,* write the first positive response you receive. **How would you explain the difference between these two pieces of information?**

Divide the class into groups of four or five. **You have ten minutes to come up with your own facts and opinions about students in our room. Fold your paper into two columns. At the top of one column, write *Facts* and at the top of the other column, write *Opinions*. Now, write down all the ideas your group can think of.** Once the groups have completed their lists, let each group share their ideas with the whole class.

Strengthening Language for Second-Language Learners

Activity 1

Objective
- to describe how people look

Materials
- Chalkboard and chalk

In the poem "Whale," the poetess used many words to describe how the whale looked. Let's list words that describe how *students* look. Encourage the students to suggest descriptive adjectives about each student's appearance. Tell the students that only positive suggestions about students will be accepted. Write these words on the chalkboard.

Activity 2

Objective
- to write and illustrate descriptive phrases

Materials
- Chalkboard and chalk
- Writing paper
- Pencils
- Drawing paper
- Crayons

On the chalkboard, write three common nouns such as *house, tree,* and *dog.* Ask the students to suggest adjectives to describe each of these things. Show how the adjectives might be combined, as in *big brown barking dog*. Have the students write and illustrate a phrase that contains a noun and at least three descriptive adjectives.

Reaching Across the Curriculum

Developing Creative Expression

Activity 1

Objective
- to write descriptive paragraphs

Materials
- Writing paper and pencils

Imagine that you are meeting someone at the movies who has never seen you before. Pretend that you're talking to that person on the telephone and you have to tell him how to recognize you. How would you describe the way you look? Write a paragraph describing your appearance. Remember, only writing "brown eyes and brown hair" isn't enough. Read some of the descriptions aloud and have the class guess who the paragraphs are describing.

Activity 2

Objective
- to create a new version of the poem

Materials
- Writing paper
- Pencils

Using the following model, have the students make up new versions of the poem.

You may find us _____ ,
You may find us _____ ,
But we would _____ :
We _____ .

Exploring Science and Art

Activity 1

Objective
- to research questions about whales

Materials
- Library sources
- Writing paper and pencils

Since whales are a fascinating subject for exploration, continue the fact-finding. Ask the students what they would like to find out about whales. Have them develop questions to be answered by their research. Discuss where the answers to their questions might be found.

Activity 2

Objective
- to create a display about whales

Materials
- Bulletin board
- Drawing paper and crayons
- Glue and newspapers

Following their research about whales, have the students create a bulletin board display about whales and their oceanic habitat. Have them draw a background ocean setting, and let them add representations of different species of whales. As an added effect, the whales could be made three-dimensional. Glue two outlines of the same shape together leaving just enough room to stuff newspaper inside the shapes.

Expanding Social Studies

Activity

Objective
- to develop increased self-acceptance

Materials
- Writing paper and pencils

How would the whale in the poem have reacted if someone had made fun of the way he looked? How do you feel about the way you look? Write a letter to someone who doesn't know you. Tell that person what you like about yourself. Be sure to include what you like about your outside *and* your inside. Help the students become more aware of who they are. Discuss how people are more than just what they look like on the outside. Explain the importance of appreciating the inner self.

Lesson 7

What Night Would It Be?

John Ciardi's spine-tingling descriptions of prowling ghosts, goblins, and witches are sure to get a reaction from your students as they visualize the scenes in this Halloween poem.

Objectives:

Students will
- develop "clues" related to holidays.
- practice choral/oral reading.
- visualize the poem's characters and events.
- appreciate the use of vivid language.
- extend language and ideas through oral and written expression.

Warming Up for Reading

Materials
- Construction paper
- Marker

On separate pieces of construction paper, write each of the following names of holidays:

Thanksgiving
Valentine's Day
Fourth of July
Halloween

Display the pieces of paper at the front of the room. **Each of these pieces of paper has a name of a holiday written on it. Let's read the names of the holidays.** Read the names aloud together.

I think you'll like the guessing game that we're going to play today because it's called "Test the Teacher." I need five volunteers to come up to the front of the room. When I turn my back, each of you should take one of the pieces of paper and bring it back to your seat. Then, I'm going to return to my seat, too. After that, each volunteer will take a turn coming to the front of the room with his paper. You should hold your piece of paper above my head so the class can see what it says, but I can't. Your challenge is to give me clues to see if I can guess the name of the holiday that's written on the piece of paper. The rest of the class can tell me if I'm right or wrong.** Play "Test the Teacher" with the class.

Today's poem is about one of the holidays that was in the game we just played. Listen closely to the poet's clues to see if you can figure out which holiday the poem is about. Don't give it away!

Sharing the Poem

Materials
- Pages 21-22 in student book

Read the poem in a mysterious, eerie voice. Stop after the first stanza and see if the students have figured out which holiday the poem is about. Then, continue reading.

What Night Would It Be?

If the moon shines
On the black pines
And an owl flies
And a ghost cries
And the hairs rise
On the back
  on the back
    on the back of your neck —

(continued)

If you look quick
At the moon-slick
On the black air
And what goes there
Rides a broom-stick
And if things pick
At the back
   at the back
      at the back of your neck —

Would you know then
By the small men
With the lit grins,
And with no chins,
By the owl's *hoo*,
And the ghost's *boo*,

By the Tom Cat,
And the Black Bat
On the night air,
And the thing there,
By the thing,
   by the thing,
      by the dark thing there

(Yes, you do,
   yes, you do
      know the thing I mean)

That it's now,
   that it's now,
      that it's — Halloween!

by John Ciardi

What kinds of pictures did you make in your head as you listened to the poem? What key words helped you figure out that the poem was about Halloween?

Turn to page 21 in your book. Look at the picture. What do you see? Turn to page 22 and look at the picture. What holiday does this picture call to mind? It's your turn to use mysterious, eerie voices as we read the poem together. Read the poem in unison. Then, divide the class into four groups. Assign each group a stanza to read aloud. Everyone

should read the last three lines of stanzas one, two, and four together. Let everyone read the last six lines of the poem together, too.

Ask the students to think of sound effects that can be added as the poem is read aloud. After reading each of the following, the students could say the suggested sound effects or others they make up.

". . . moon shines" o-o-o-o-o-o
". . . owl flies" hoo-hoo-hoo
". . . broom stick" swish, swish

After the students have agreed on the sound effects, break the class into two groups. Have one group read the poem aloud while the second group provides the sound effects. For subsequent readings, have the whole class read the poem aloud with the sound effects assigned to individual students.

Putting Ideas to Work

Things to Talk About

Material
• Page 23 in student book

Look at page 23 in your book. "Things to Talk About" asks us to do some thinking about scary things.

Read the first question with me. "How does the poet help you create pictures in your mind?"

Some possible student responses
a. He tells you all the things he sees.
b. He tells you all the things he feels.
c. He uses words that make pictures in your mind.

Read the second question with me. "What do you think the 'dark thing' mentioned in the poem could be?"

Some possible student responses — a ghost, a witch, a monster

Read the third question with me. "What makes 'the hairs rise on the back . . . of *your* neck'?" What makes you so scared or

anxious that it feels like the hairs on the back of your neck are sticking straight up?

Some possible student responses — scary movies, creepy noises, dark rooms

Read the fourth question with me. "What makes Halloween a favorite day of the year?"

Some possible student responses
a. You get to dress up in neat costumes.
b. You get to go trick-or-treating.
c. You get to scare people.

Things to Do

Materials
- Page 23 in student book
- Writing paper
- Pencils
- Drawing paper
- Crayons

Look at the "Things to Do" on page 23 in your book. Ask each student to choose one of the four activities to do, or pick one for the whole class to do. Please note that, in this instance, the second and third activities are extensions of the first activity.

Let's read number 1 together. "Make a list of Halloween words that aren't in the poem. Compare your list with a friend's." Have the students write lists of Halloween words.

Let's read number 2 together. "Use words from your Halloween word list to write your own rhyme." Make up a short poem about Halloween. Try to use as many words from your Halloween word list as you can. Have the students write poems about Halloween.

Let's read number 3 together. "Using words from your Halloween word list, write a short paragraph that tells what happens on Halloween night in your neighborhood." Have the students write paragraphs about Halloween.

Let's read number 4 together. "Find the description in the poem that you like best.

Draw that part of the poem." Have the students illustrate parts of the poem.

Extending Language and Thinking

Activity

Objectives
- to discuss story elements
- to devise solutions to problems
- to create stories using these elements

Materials
- Chalkboard and chalk
- Writing paper
- Pencils
- Drawing paper
- Crayons
- Bulletin board

On the chalkboard, draw four columns. At the top of each column, write one of the following: *Character, Setting, Halloween Problem,* and *Solution.*

Today, we're going to write our own spooky Halloween stories! On your paper, copy the information that I've written on the chalkboard. You'll be using this chart to create your story *skeleton*. I'll show you how to do it.

On the chalkboard, write your name under *Character*. For my story, *I'm* going to be the main character. Now, I need to decide on the *setting,* or where the action of my story will take place. Do you have any ideas? Elicit the students' responses and write one of the ideas under *Setting*. Then, explain that they are to imagine some kind of problem you might encounter in your Halloween story. Write one of their ideas under *Halloween Problem.*

We'll leave the *Solution* column blank for now. It's time for you to work on your own story skeletons. On their papers, have the students fill in the columns labeled *Character, Setting,* and *Halloween Problem* with their own ideas.

Once the students have finished, direct their attention again to the chart on the chalkboard. Ask the students to suggest possible solutions to the problem written there. Write a sensible solution under the fourth column. Then, divide the class into pairs. Have each pair exchange papers. Have each student suggest a possible solution to his partner's problem. Tell him to write it on his partner's paper in column four. Give each pair an opportunity to discuss the solutions suggested.

Have the students use the information in their story skeletons to write paragraphs describing the action and events. Once rough drafts have been completed, have the students share their work in small groups. Instruct the groups to share both what they liked about the paragraphs and what they think could be changed to improve them.

Provide time for the students to revise their paragraphs. Have them recopy the paragraphs neatly and illustrate them. Post the students' work on a "Spooky Stories" bulletin board.

Strengthening Language for Second-Language Learners

Activity 1

Objectives
- to promote sight-word recognition
- to practice word association

Materials
- Chalkboard and chalk
- Index cards
- Markers

On the chalkboard, write the following lists of words:

owl	witch
ghost	shines
moon	hoo
broomstick	boo

Pronounce each word carefully, and have the students repeat it. Then, have the students copy each word onto an index card. Ask each student

to arrange the cards in two rows on his desk, in the order that the words are written on the chalkboard.

Which word in the right-hand column goes with _owl?_ Once the students have provided the correct answer, draw a line on the chalkboard from _owl_ to _hoo_. Discuss why these two words go together. Ask each student to place the card with _hoo_ written on it underneath the _owl_ card. Continue this procedure until all words have been matched and discussed.

Activity 2

Objective
- to use words in sentences

Material
- List of words from **Activity 1**

Point to a word on the chalkboard, and call on a student to use that word in a sentence. (For example, **The _witch_ looked mean.**) Continue this activity until all the words have been used in sentences.

Then, have the students make up sentences using each of the matched pairs on the chalkboard. (For example, **The _witch_ rode on a _broomstick_**).

Reaching Across the Curriculum

Expanding Social Studies

Activity 1

Objective
- to summarize information about certain holidays

Materials
- Chalkboard and chalk
- Writing paper
- Pencils

On the chalkboard, write the following chart.

	Special Foods	No School	Costumes	Parades	Celebrate with Favorite People
Halloween					
Valentine's Day					
Fourth of July					
Thanksgiving					

Divide the class into small groups. Have each group select one member to copy the chart. Have the groups discuss the holidays in terms of the categories on the chart. Have the students put a + in the box if the item at the top of the chart applies to the holiday and a – if it doesn't. Since some discrepancies may come up, let the students know that they may have a + and a – in the same box. Tell them to put a ? when they are unsure.

Once the groups have completed their charts, discuss their decisions and record them on the chart on the chalkboard. Then, ask the students to summarize their findings. If necessary, point out that different people observe holidays in different ways and that some people do not observe certain holidays at all.

Activity 2

Objective
- to research a holiday

Materials
- Library sources
- Writing paper and pencils

Divide the class into groups. Ask each group to research the origin of a nationally recognized holiday. Then, have them present their findings to the rest of the class.

Expanding Literature

Activity

Objective
- to share a poem and illustrate it

Materials
- Drawing paper and crayons

Read the following "oldie but goodie" to the students. Ask them to listen carefully to the words and phrases that describe the character.

Queen Nefertiti

Spin a coin, spin a coin,
    All fall down;
Queen Nefertiti
    Stalks through the town.

Over the pavements,
    Her feet go clack.
Her legs are as tall
    As a chimney stack.

Her fingers flicker
    Like snakes in the air.
The walls split open
    At her green-eyed stare.

Her voice is thin
    As the ghosts of bees.
She will crumble your bones.
    She will make your blood freeze.

Spin a coin, spin a coin,
    All fall down;
Queen Nefertiti
    Stalks through the town.
        Anonymous

What kind of person is Queen Nefertiti? Is she dangerous? How do you know?

Do you remember what Queen Nefertiti looks like? Listen carefully as I read the poem a second time because when I'm through, you get to draw pictures of this mysterious woman.

Lesson 8

Pirate Don Durk of Dowdee

Your classroom will never be the same after this swashbuckling buccaneer visits! How is it possible to be *so* wicked and yet *so* charming? The colorful language and descriptions will captivate your students.

Objectives:

Students will
- listen for clues on which to base predictions.
- practice choral/oral reading.
- recall details from the poem.
- recognize vividly descriptive language.
- extend language and ideas through oral and written expression.

Warming Up for Reading

Materials
- Chalkboard and chalk
- Writing paper
- Pencils

On the chalkboard, write *Can you guess our guest?*

You know how we sometimes invite people to visit our class? Well, today you're in for an *extraordinary* surprise! Our guest looks and acts very different from anyone you've ever met before. I guarantee you'll enjoy our unusual visitor. See if you can figure out what kind of work he does. Don't yell out if you think you can guess his occupation. *Write* down what you think he does, and keep it a secret. Here are some clues.

1. **This guest travels a lot.**
2. **His line of work does not make him very popular.**
3. **He often gets involved in violent situations.**
4. **He dresses in a very colorful outfit.**
5. **He spends more time on water than on land.**

Any ideas as to who our visitor is? Write them down. See if you have correctly identified today's guest. Here comes the one and only, the daring and devilish, the evil man of the seas, Don Durk of Dowdee!

Sharing the Poem

Materials
- Pages 24-25 in student book
- Simple props

Read the poem with exaggerated expression.

(Turn the page for the poem.)

Pirate Don Durk of Dowdee

Ho, for the Pirate Don Durk of Dowdee!
He was as wicked as wicked could be,
But oh, he was perfectly gorgeous to see!
   The Pirate Don Durk of Dowdee.

His conscience, of course, was black as a bat,
But he had a floppety plume on his hat
And when he went walking it jiggled — like that!
   The plume of the Pirate Dowdee.

His coat it was crimson and cut with a slash,
And often as ever he twirled his moustache,
Deep down in the ocean the mermaids went splash,
   Because of Don Durk of Dowdee.

Moreover, Dowdee had a purple tattoo,
And stuck in his belt where he buckled it through
Were a dagger, a dirk and a squizzamaroo
   For fierce was the Pirate Dowdee.

So fearful he was he would shoot at a puff,
And always at sea when the weather grew rough
He drank from a bottle and wrote on his cuff,
   Did Pirate Don Durk of Dowdee.

Oh, he had a cutlass that swung at his thigh
And he had a parrot called Pepperkin Pye,
And a zigzaggy scar at the end of his eye
   Had Pirate Don Durk of Dowdee.

He kept in a cavern, this buccaneer bold,
A curious chest that was covered with mould,
And all of his pockets were jingly with gold!
   Oh, jing! went the gold of Dowdee.

His conscience, of course, it was crook'd like a squash,
But both of his boots made a slickery slosh,
And he went through the world with a wonderful swash,
   Did Pirate Don Durk of Dowdee.

It's true he was wicked as wicked could be,
His sins they outnumbered a hundred and three,
But oh, he was perfectly gorgeous to see,
   The Pirate Don Durk of Dowdee.

   by Mildred Meigs

Did you guess that our guest would be a pirate? Although Don Durk could not be with us in person, he's very proud of this poem written in his honor. He feels the poem captures a bit of his spirit, although he claims he's not as bad as the poem makes him out to be. What do you think? The poem describes him so vividly that we can almost imagine that Don Durk *is here in this room.* What was he wearing? What did you find out about him? Encourage the students to recall details from the poem.

Turn to page 24 in your book. Look at the picture on page 25. How does Don Durk seem to feel about himself? Does he look like you had imagined? I know Don Durk would be pleased if we all joined in and read the poem together. For now, follow along as I read, and join in on the fourth line of each stanza.

Which words in the poem describe the way the pirate looked? Which words describe how he acted? Those action words are important because we need to select someone to pantomime the pirate's actions as we each read a stanza. Select one student to act out the pirate's motions and nine students to read individual stanzas. The whole class should chime in on the fourth line of each stanza.

This poem provides excellent material for a Reader's Theater presentation for another class, especially with a "pirate" pantomiming the words. Props and a costume would add to the effect.

Putting Ideas to Work

Things to Talk About

Materials
- Page 26 in student book
- Chalkboard and chalk

Look at page 26 in your book. "Things to Talk About" asks us to do some thinking about pirates.

Read number 1 with me. "Which parts of the poem tell you something about the personality of the pirate?" Look at the poem again. Find the words and phrases that tell about Don Durk's personality. What are they? Write the students' responses on the chalkboard.

Some possible student responses
a. "wicked as wicked could be"
b. "fierce"
c. "bold"

Read number 2 with me. "The poem talks about the pirate's conscience. What is a conscience? Why was it 'black as a bat' and 'crook'd like a squash'? What do you think made it that way?"

Some possible student responses
A conscience helps you tell right from wrong.
a. The pirate stole from people.
b. The pirate got in lots of fights.
c. The pirate's "sins they outnumbered a hundred and three."
The pirate was probably never taught what is right and what is wrong.

Read number 3 with me. "Why are people fascinated with pirates?" Lead a class discussion about the myths and realities of pirates' lives.

Some possible student responses
a. Pirates' lives are full of adventure.
b. Pirates find buried treasure.
c. Pirates travel on all the oceans of the world.

Things to Do

Materials

- Page 26 in student book
- Writing paper
- Pencils
- Drawing paper
- Crayons

Look at the "Things to Do" on page 26 in your book. Ask each student to choose one of the three activities to do, or pick one for the whole class to do.

Let's read number 1 together. "The poem says that the pirate's sins 'outnumbered a hundred and three.' Describe in detail *one* of the wicked things that Pirate Don Durk might have done." Have the students describe Pirate Don Durk's wicked deeds.

Let's read number 2 together. "Make up five questions that you would like to ask the pirate if you were to meet him face-to-face. Write the questions on a sheet of paper." Have the students make up questions that they would like to ask the pirate.

Let's read number 3 together. "Based on the vivid description in the poem, draw a picture of the Pirate Don Durk of Dowdee." Have the students draw their own versions of the pirate.

Extending Language and Thinking

Activity 1

Objective

- to create a class-composed story

Materials

- Duplicating master
- Writing paper
- Pencils

On the chalkboard, write the following story starter.

One dark and stormy night, the Pirate Don Durk of Dowdee and his gallant ship, the _____ , were barely able to keep afloat when out of nowhere came the sound of a _____ .

Have one student come to the chalkboard, and have her fill in the blanks. Then, ask the students to continue the story. Give a piece of paper to a student, and ask her to add one sentence of her own. After she's finished, have her pass the paper to the person sitting on her right. Have that person read what has already been written and then add a sentence of her own.

After a specified time, read the group-created story aloud. Make any corrections necessary. Then, have a student recopy the story on a duplicating master so that each student can have a copy. Discuss ways to improve the story, and make further changes if necessary.

Activity 2

Objective

- to create descriptive paragraphs about characters

Materials

- Writing paper
- Pencils

This poem uses vivid language to create a colorful picture of a character. Ask the students to select an exciting character, living or dead, real or make-believe. Have them make lists of details that help create pictures of the individuals that they have chosen. Then, have the students write descriptive paragraphs about their characters. Challenge them to use rich language that creates visual images.

Strengthening Language
for Second-Language Learners

Activity 1

Objectives
- to paraphrase the stanzas of the poem
- to illustrate the stanzas
- to sequence the illustrations

Materials
- Drawing paper
- Crayons

After discussing the character and theme of this poem, ask the students to paraphrase each stanza in their own words. Then, have each student select one stanza to illustrate. As you read each stanza, have a student hold up the illustration that matches.

Activity 2

Objective
- to pantomime the actions of the poem

Materials
- Pages 24-25 in student book

To reinforce comprehension of the language, encourage the students to act out parts of the poem by pointing to parts of their bodies and making appropriate facial expressions and motions.

Reaching Across the Curriculum

Developing Creative Expression

Activity

Objective
- to create a life-size pirate

Materials
- Large piece of paper
- Markers
- Simple props for the pirate

The vivid descriptions in this poem lend themselves to illustration. Have one student lie down on the large piece of paper. Trace the outline of her body. Use this outline to make a life-size Pirate Don Durk. Let each student contribute to the group project by adding something from the poem. The following real materials could be added: plumes, a yarn moustache, a bottle, a treasure chest, gold foil money, jewels, a foil dagger, etc. The Pirate Don Durk look-alike could accompany a class presentation of the poem.

Expanding Social Studies

Activity

Objective
- to do research on pirates

Materials
- Library sources

The following questions provide a basis for interesting research. **Who were some *real* pirates? What does "privateer" mean? What are some real places associated with pirates? Are there any records of pirates who exist today?**

Expanding Literature

Activity

Objective
- to share pirate stories and poems

Materials
- Library books

Pirates are a source of excitement and enjoyment. Go on a class "treasure hunt" to find stories and poems about pirates. Let the students take turns sharing their stories or poems with the rest of the class.

Lesson 9

Beware Where You Sit

Did you know that the act of sitting could be hazardous to one's health? This will be clearly demonstrated to your students as they tongue-trip through "Beware Where You Sit." This comical poem describes the zany antics of some capricious characters.

Objectives:

Students will

- relate personal experiences to the theme of the poem.
- identify significant events and details.
- practice choral/oral reading.
- identify the pattern of the poem and write their own limericks.
- extend language and ideas through oral and written expression.

Warming Up for Reading

Materials

- Chalkboard and chalk

On the chalkboard, write *Beware where you sit.*

Was there ever a time when you sat down without looking and got a surprise, like sitting on something you didn't expect to be there? I remember one time when I . . . Share a personal experience, or make one up. **Now, tell about a time when something like this happened to you.** Have the students share their experiences.

You'll really be surprised when you hear about the careless characters in the poem today. They obviously didn't heed the warning given in the chorus of the poem. Be listening to see who you think got the biggest surprise.

Sharing the Poem

Materials

- Pages 27-28 in student book

Read the poem aloud encouraging the students to join in by chanting the chorus.

(Turn the page for the poem.)

Beware Where You Sit

Be careful before you sit down.
    Who knows what you'll find on the ground?
Beware where you sit,
    Or you may just get bit
By something that's hanging around!

Mr. Simon LaTeath of Blackheath
    Sat down on his set of false teeth.
    Said he, with a start,
"Oh my, bless my heart!
I've bitten myself underneath!"

Mrs. Amy Von Drake of Fonlake
    Sat down on a large rattlesnake.
    Said she, with a start,
"Oh my, bless my heart!
Its fangs are as sharp as a rake!"

Be careful before you sit down.
    Who knows what you'll find on the ground?
Beware where you sit,
    Or you may just get bit
By something that's hanging around!

Young Wilbur Wettfine of Shoreline
    Sat down on a small porcupine.
    Said he, with a start,
"Oh my, bless my heart!
I'm feeling some pain down behind."

Miss Mandy Highstyle of Grandfile
    Sat down on a huge crocodile.
    Said she, with a start,
"Oh my, bless my heart!
I believe that this rock has a smile!"

Be careful before you sit down.
    Who knows what you'll find on the ground?
Beware where you sit,
    Or you may just get bit
By something that's hanging around!

    by Maurice Poe

Which of these characters do you think got the biggest surprise? What were the other surprises? What lesson do you think the characters learned?

Turn to page 27 in your book. Look at the picture. Who sat on this? Turn to page 28 and look at the picture. What did this character just do? How do you think he feels? Let's read the chorus aloud together in a warning voice. Lead the students in practicing the chorus.

Now, find the part that Mr. LaTeath says aloud. Let's read what he says. Read the part in quotation marks with an excited expression in your voices. Then, lead the class in practicing reading aloud the exclamations of Mrs. Von Drake, Wilbur Wettfine, and Mandy Highstyle.

Now, we're ready to read the poem from beginning to end! Guide the students in reading the poem in unison.

Let's read the poem again. We'll need students to play the roles of LaTeath, Von Drake, Wettfine, and Highstyle. We'll need narrators to read the lines that come before each character's words, and the rest of us will chant the chorus. Assign various reading roles to the students, and have the class read the poem aloud. For subsequent readings, the students can take turns playing the roles of the various characters in the selection.

Putting Ideas to Work

Things to Talk About

Material
• Page 29 in student book

Look at page 29 in your book. "Things to Talk About" asks us to do some thinking about the people in the poem.

Read the first question with me. "Why didn't the characters in the poem look around before they sat down?"

Some possible student responses
a. They didn't think anything dangerous would be underneath them.
b. Someone or something was distracting them.
c. They forgot to look around.

Read the second set of questions with me. "Which person sat on the most dangerous thing? Why do you think that was the most dangerous?"

Some possible student responses
a. Mrs. Amy Von Drake — A rattlesnake is poisonous.
b. Miss Mandy Highstyle — A crocodile can swallow you up.

Read the third set of questions with me. "Which person sat on the most harmless thing? Why do you think that was the most harmless?"

Some possible student responses
a. Mr. Simon LaTeath — His false teeth probably aren't very sharp.
b. Young Wilbur Wettfine — The porcupine was small.

Read the fourth set of questions with me. "What is ridiculous about the poem? What is realistic?"

Some possible student responses
Ridiculous — Mandy Highstyle sat down on a huge crocodile.
Realistic — Simon LaTeath sat down on his false teeth.

Things to Do

Materials
• Page 29 in student book
• Drawing paper
• Crayons
• Writing paper
• Pencils

Look at the "Things to Do" on page 29 in your book. Ask each student to choose one of the three activities to do, or pick one for the whole class to do.

Let's read number 1 together. "Draw two pictures of one of the characters in the poem. Have one picture show the character *before* sitting down and the other show the character *after* sitting down." Fold your paper in half. On one half, write *Before*. Draw a picture of one of the characters *before* sitting down. On the other half, write *After*. Draw a picture of the character *after* sitting down. Have the students draw *before* and *after* pictures of the poem's characters.

Let's read number 2 together. "Write a story that describes what happens to one of the characters in the poem *after* sitting on something unexpected." Have the students write stories about the poem's characters.

Let's read number 3 together. "Finish the following poem with your own words. Be sure that lines a., b., and e. rhyme and contain the same number of beats. Also, make lines c. and d. rhyme and contain the same number of beats."

Copy the poem below these directions on your paper. Leave blank spaces just like in your book. Once you have finished copying the poem, you should begin to fill in the blanks with your own words. Remember, lines a., b., and e. should rhyme. They should also contain the same number of beats. Also, try to make lines c. and d. rhyme and contain the same number of beats. Good luck! Have the students complete the poem. Give individual help if necessary.

Extending Language and Thinking

Activity 1

Objective
• to identify objects that are dangerous to sit on

Materials
• Writing paper
• Pencils
• Chalkboard and chalk

This poem describes some characters who were not very careful about *where* they sat or *what* they sat on. Let's see if we can think of other things that would be hazardous to sit on. I'll divide you into groups. Think of all the things that would be dangerous to sit on, and write them down on your paper. When you're finished, we'll compare your lists. Divide the class into groups of four or five students and allow enough time for exchanging and recording ideas.

Now, it's sharing time. Raise your hands if your group came up with at least three dangerous objects to sit on. Did anyone come up with four or five or more? Congratulations!

Listen carefully as each group shares their list. On your paper, place a check mark in front of any item that another group reads, so that when your group shares, you read the names of any item that has *not* been mentioned by any other group. On the chalkboard, record the items identified by the students. After all the groups have shared their lists, have the students examine the list on the chalkboard. Ask them to consider if there are any objects listed that do *not* pose a danger to someone's health and well-being.

Activity 2

Objectives
• to locate rhyming words in the poem
• to write sentences using rhyming words

Materials
• Writing paper
• Pencils

Have the students examine the poem and find groups of rhyming words such as LaTeath, Blackheath, teeth, and underneath. Record the rhyming words on paper. Challenge the students to use each group of rhyming words in a single sentence without duplicating the exact sentence from the poem. (For example, *Simon LaTeath of the town of Blackheath sat down on his false teeth, which produced pain underneath.*) Provide an opportunity for each student to share his sentence with the class.

Activity 3

Objectives
- to add to the rhyming words in the poem
- to use the new rhyming words in sentences

Materials
- Writing paper
- Pencils

Divide the class into groups of four or five students. Each group should select a rhyming pattern from the poem and list as many additional rhyming words as they can in a given period of time. After the students have generated a list of words for the rhyming pattern selected, challenge them to use as many of the *new* rhyming words as they can in a sentence that makes sense. Here is an example.

Rhyming words from poem
Highstyle	Grandfile
crocodile	smile

New rhyming words
mile	aisle	while	tile
trial	file	style	Nile

Sentence
> She lost her *file while* walking down the *aisle* at her *trial,* which was held a *mile* from the *Nile.*

Strengthening Language for Second-Language Learners

Activity 1

Objectives
- to understand the usage of *sat* and *sit*
- to strengthen sight-word recognition
- to practice using sight words in sentences

Materials
- Chalkboard and chalk
- Index cards
- Markers

The present and past tenses of verbs often pose problems for *all* speakers and writers of the English language. This poem presents an opportunity to immerse learners in distinguishing between the uses of *sat* and *sit*.

On the chalkboard, write *sit, sat, sits,* and *sitting.* Have the students write these words on index cards, and tell them to place the cards in front of them. Read the following sentences aloud asking each student to hold up the appropriate card that matches the verb in that sentence.

1. I will *sit* next to Tom.
2. He has *sat* there every day.
3. He always *sits* quietly.
4. Where were you *sitting* in the auditorium?
5. You may *sit* down now.
6. Irma *sat* with her hands folded.
7. Mark is *sitting* in my seat.
8. Carolyn *sits* next to Fran in the cafeteria every day.

To continue the exercise, point to a form of *sit* on the chalkboard. Call on a student to say a sentence using this word.

Activity 2

Objectives
- to understand the usage of *sit* and *set*
- to strengthen sight-word recognition

Materials
- Index cards
- Markers
- Word cards for *sit* and *sat* from **Activity 1**

You may also wish to have the students distinguish between the use of *sit* and *set, sit* meaning "to rest" and *set* meaning "to put or place."

Have each student make an additional card containing the word *set.* Tell the students to place the cards *sit, sat,* and *set* in front of them. Read the following sentences aloud asking each student to hold up the appropriate card that matches the verb in that sentence.

1. Bill *sat* still and said nothing.
2. Please *set* the book on the table.
3. If you *sit* on the ground, you may get wet.
4. The chairs were *set* next to the wall.
5. Someone *sat* in the fresh paint.
6. Margaret *set* her books on my desk.

Reaching Across the Curriculum

Expanding Literature

Activity

Objective
- to share a book of limericks

Material
- Children's book
  Lear, Edward. *A Book of Nonsense*. New York: The Viking Press, 1980.

Students of all ages delight in listening to humorous limericks. Most libraries have several volumes containing this poetry form. A good source for limericks is *A Book of Nonsense* by Edward Lear. This work contains many knee-slapping limericks that will entertain your students and immerse them in language.

Developing Creative Expression

Activity

Objectives
- to foster understanding of limericks
- to create limericks

Materials
- Chalkboard and chalk
- Writing paper
- Pencils

After the class has read several limericks, write one of your favorite limericks on the chalkboard. Emphasize the form of the limerick. Explain that the first, second, and fifth lines rhyme and usually have the same number of beats. The third and fourth lines are shorter but rhyme and contain the same number of beats. Then, write the following limerick on the chalkboard.

There was a young lady named Flo	*a*	*(8)*
Who couldn't get flowers to _____	*a*	*(8)*
She planted some seeds	*b*	*(5)*
But only grew _____	*b*	*(5)*
What happened I really don't _____.	*a*	*(8)*

Using the letters *a* and *b*, label the lines indicating the rhyme pattern. Write the number of beats per line. Ask the students to suggest rhyming words to complete each unfinished sentence in the limerick. Leave the model on the chalkboard, and ask the students to write and share their own limericks.

Expanding Social Studies

Activity 1

Objective
- to discuss hazards of practical jokes

Material
- None

Practical jokers often place things on desk seats, bleachers, chairs, and car and bus seats. Lead a class discussion on the dangers of such behavior. **What might happen if a dangerous object were placed on a car seat? on a bleacher seat? What kind of personal injuries might result?** Help the students understand that practical jokes can lead to personal injuries such as blood poisoning, punctures, or cuts that can cause infection.

Practical jokers are famous for pulling the chair out from under a person about to sit down. Discuss the hazards of such behavior.

Activity 2

Objective
- to create safety posters

Materials
- Drawing paper
- Markers
- Bulletin board

We've discussed how important paying attention to where we sit is to our health and safety. Now, let's make some safety posters. First, write *Be Careful Where You Sit* at the top of your paper. Then, draw a picture that shows a person about to sit on something dangerous. The posters can be placed on bulletin boards in the classroom and around the school.

Lesson 10

Neat Feet

Shopping expeditions sometimes lead to conflict. Your students will easily identify with the desire for "dream sneakers" in this playful rhyme.

Objectives:

Students will
- discuss personal experiences related to theme of poem.
- practice choral/oral reading.
- identify emotional reactions.
- develop persuasive arguments.
- use theme of poem in creative written expression.
- extend language and ideas through oral and written expression.

Warming Up for Reading

Material
- None

Have any of you bought new shoes lately? What happened when you went to the store to get them? Did you get your first choice? Who took you shopping? Did you agree on the ones you would get? Guide the students in a discussion about shoe shopping.

I remember always wearing out my shoes and needing a new pair, but what I wanted to buy was sometimes different from what my mom had in mind. Has this ever happened to you? See if you have ever had an experience like the boy in the poem.

Sharing the Poem

Materials
- Pages 30-31 in student book

Read the poem aloud with expression. Encourage the students to snap their fingers rhythmically to the chorus of the poem.

Neat Feet

**New shoes, two shoes, gotta go and buy 'em.
Neat feet, beat feet, try 'em on and tie 'em.**

My mama said, "Are those your toes?
New shoes again? We just got those!"
She grabbed me, pushed me out the door,
And drove right to the mall shoe store.

She went inside, began to speak,
"Remember us? Was just last week.
We bought a pair. I do declare!
This child will drive me to despair!"

"Aw, Mom," I said, "I had to hike,
And then I ripped them on my bike.
Was it my fault? I'm not to blame.
They took a beating in the game."

**New shoes, two shoes, gotta go and buy 'em.
Neat feet, beat feet, try 'em on and tie 'em.**

The shoe man sighed, "What size today?"
Then he began to turn away.
My mama said, "A size that's cheap!"
He pointed to some in a heap.

(continued)

And then I saw them lying there,
The kind I could wear anywhere!
Wild black and silver, made for speed.
Dream sneakers — just the kind I need.

Dots of orange with stripes of green,
The meanest running shoes I've seen.
I'd lead the pack with those shoes on.
I'd win the Boston Marathon.

New shoes, two shoes, gotta go and buy 'em.
Neat feet, beat feet, try 'em on and tie 'em.

I sauntered over, played it cool.
My mom said, "Boy, don't be a fool!
Get your hands off those flashy feet,
Or you'll be shoeless in the street."

I made a face. Mom turned to see
Some boring shoes he brought to me.
Could Mom not tell I'd win my fame?
Those 'rageous sneaks just called my name!

While Mama's back was turned I sat
And pulled them on in seconds flat.
A little snug but not too tight.
Then Mama said, "He'll take the WHITE!"

New shoes, two shoes, gotta go and buy 'em.
Neat feet, beat feet, try 'em on and tie 'em.

by Barbara Schmidt

Was there anything familiar about this poem? Did the mother remind you of anyone? What kind of sneakers do you think the boy gets in the end? What does " 'rageous" mean?

Turn to page 30 in your book. Look at the picture. Is this what you pictured "dream sneakers" would look like? Look at the pictures of the boy on page 31. Why is he smiling? Read along silently as I go through the poem again. The chorus has a good rhythmic beat. You do the chorus part each time I get to it.

After guiding the students through the poem, a group reading can take place. Repeated readings can involve the students taking the part of the young boy, the mother, and the narrator. The students with these roles can dramatize the actions of the poem while the rest of the class snaps, claps, taps, and chants to the chorus.

Putting Ideas to Work

Things to Talk About

Material
• Page 32 in student book

Look at page 32 in your book. "Things to Talk About" tells us to do some thinking about new shoes.

Read the first question with me. "What kind of shoes did the boy in this poem want to buy?"

Possible student response — black and silver sneakers with orange dots and green stripes

Read the second question with me. "Why did 'Mama' object to the dream sneakers?" Why do you think Mama wouldn't buy the dream sneakers?

Some possible student responses
a. The dream sneakers were too expensive.
b. She thought the dream sneakers were ugly.
c. She thought the dream sneakers would be out of style soon, and her son wouldn't like them anymore.

Read the third question with me. "How do you think the boy feels when he's leaving the shoe store?"

Some possible student responses — sad, disappointed, angry

Read the fourth question with me. "How could you have convinced 'Mama' to let you buy the sneakers?" Pretend you're the boy in the poem. Your mother wants to buy you boring white sneakers instead of the " 'rageous" pair of dream sneakers you have your eye on. What could you do or say to convince her that you should have those dream sneakers?

Some possible student responses
a. I'd tell her that I'd be extra careful with my new sneakers so they'd last a long time.
b. I'd tell her that if she'd buy me the dream sneakers, I'd make her dinner for a week.
c. I'd tell her that I'd never ask her for anything again.

Things to Do

Materials
- Page 32 in student book
- Writing paper
- Pencils

Look at the "Things to Do" on page 32 in your book. Ask each student to choose one of the three activities to do, or pick one for the whole class to do.

Let's read number 1 together. "Describe your favorite pair of shoes. What makes them special? Describe a pair of shoes you dislike. How are the two pairs different?" Have the students describe and compare their favorite shoes with a pair they dislike.

Let's read number 2 together. "Write a story describing an adventure you might have with a pair of amazing sneakers with magical powers. Tell about where the sneakers would take you and what would happen." Have the students write about their imagined adventures.

Let's read number 3 together. "Ask your parents or grandparents what kind of shoes they wore when they were young. List some advantages sneakers have compared to the shoes that your parents or grandparents wore." Have the students compare sneakers to shoes that their parents or grandparents wore.

Extending Language and Thinking
Activity

Objective
- to write descriptions of "wants"

Materials
- Chalkboard and chalk
- Writing paper
- Pencils

Was there ever a time when you wanted to buy something that your parents wouldn't allow? Were you able to convince them to let you buy it?

On the chalkboard, write the following sentence frame.

One time I wanted _____ but _____
_____ .

Complete this sentence on your paper. Tell us what it was that you wanted. As you write, be sure to use details to describe what it was and why you wanted it. Tell us how your parents reacted. Why did they say no? What happened? After the students have had an opportunity to write their descriptions, allow time for individual sharing.

Strengthening Language for Second-Language Learners

Activity 1

Objectives
- to describe kinds of sneakers
- to name different kinds of shoes

Materials
- Chalkboard and chalk

On the chalkboard, write *sneakers*. Point to a pair of sneakers that a student is wearing. Ask the students to describe a pair of sneakers using words that tell about the color(s), the materials, the size, and why children like to wear them. Then, encourage the students to name different kinds of shoes in their first language. Write these words on the chalkboard.

Activity 2

Objective
- to discuss shopping trips

Material
- None

Encourage the students to talk about shopping trips. Where do they go? Whom do they go with? What do they buy?

Reaching Across the Curriculum

Developing Creative Expression

Activity

Objective
- to write a creative story

Materials
- Chalkboard and chalk
- Writing paper
- Pencils

On the chalkboard, write *A Day in the Life of a Sneaker.*

Put yourself in the place of your shoes. Imagine that you are poor beat-up sneakers. Write about your day from the minute you get put on until you get thrown onto the floor at night. Where do you go? What do you feel? What adventures do you have?

Expanding Social Studies

Activity

Objectives
- to research types of shoes
- to illustrate types of shoes

Materials
- Library sources
- Drawing paper
- Crayons

Sneakers are common footwear today, but throughout history people have worn a variety of different shoes. With your students, brainstorm a list of the kinds of shoes worn now or in the past. Encourage the students to research additional types of shoes to add to the list. Have the students illustrate different types of shoes and investigate why certain shoes are useful for different climates and purposes.

Exploring Science

Activity

Objective
- to research sneakers

Materials
- Library sources

We take sneakers for granted, but some professional athletes are dependent on the quality of their shoes. Encourage the students to find out what they can about sneakers. Have them do research on the different kinds, what to look for in a good fit, proper care, etc.

Lesson 11

On Top of Spaghetti

An adventuresome meatball offers opportunities to chant and sing this familiar favorite.

Objectives:

Students will
- use clues to identify a food.
- practice choral/oral reading.
- chant expressively with appropriate gestures.
- relate personal experiences.
- use imagination and content of poem to create illustrations.
- use the patterns of the poem to create an alternative version.
- extend language and ideas through oral and written expression.

Warming Up for Reading

Material
- None

We're going to play a "Use the Clues" game today. You need to listen carefully to guess what our poem is about. I'll give you five clues. Raise your hand when you *think* you know what it is. I won't tell you if you guessed right until we hear all five clues. That way everybody has a chance to do some good thinking. Here we go with clue number one. Our poem is about a favorite food that most children like to eat. Do you think you know? Encourage student responses to this question and to those that follow.

Listen to clue number two. Sometimes this food is messy and hard to pick up on your fork. Now, who thinks they know? Here's clue number three. When I was little, I had a hard time saying the name of this food. Are there any more guesses? Listen for the last two clues to find out if you guessed right. Here is clue number four. This food comes in funny, long, slippery strings. Can you guess? Here's the last clue. Sometimes you can eat this food with meatballs and with cheese sprinkled on top. Did you guess . . . *spaghetti?*

You did a fine job of figuring out the clues. Maybe that's because you've eaten spaghetti, and you like it. Well, the person in our poem also likes spaghetti, but something awful happens right in the middle of eating. Listen to this spaghetti adventure.

Sharing the Poem

Material
- Page 33 in student book

Read the poem dramatically, looking dismal when the meatball gets away. Then, sing it to the tune of "On Top of Old Smokey."

On Top of Spaghetti

On top of spaghetti,
All covered with cheese,
I lost my poor meatball,
When somebody sneezed.

(continued)

It rolled off the table
And onto the floor,
And then my poor meatball
Rolled out of the door.

It rolled in the garden,
And under a bush,
And then my poor meatball
Was nothing but mush.

The mush was as tasty
As tasty could be,
And early that summer,
It grew to a tree.

The tree was all covered
With beautiful moss,
It grew great big meatballs,
And tomato sauce.

So if you eat spaghetti,
All covered with cheese,
Hold onto your meatball,
And don't ever sneeze. (Ah-h-h-choo!)

by Tom Glazer

What happened to ruin this spaghetti dinner? What happened to the meatball? I've never seen a meatball tree. I think the person who wrote this poem is teasing us. It would be fun to have a tree that could grow our favorite foods, like a pizza tree, a fried chicken tree, or a taco tree. What other kinds of trees can you think of?

After we have some fun with our spaghetti poem, we can make up some crazy food trees. Now, help me out with our poem. What made the meatball roll off the table and onto the floor? When I come to that part of the poem, give me an "Ah-h-h-choo!" Read the poem again, asking the students to chime in with sneezes.

Find your own spaghetti and meatball poem on page 33 in your book. Look at the picture. What's running away? Is this how you imagined it would look? Read the first stanza with me. For further readings, have the class read the poem together several times trying out facial expressions and gestures to go with each stanza.

Putting Ideas to Work

Things to Talk About

Material
• Page 34 in student book

Look at page 34 in your book. "Things to Talk About" asks us to do some thinking about the poem.

Read number 1 with me. "What's ridiculous about this poem?"

Some possible student responses
a. A sneeze knocked the meatball on the floor.
b. The meatball mush grew into a tree.
c. The tree grew meatballs and tomato sauce.

Read number 2 with me. "How do you think the person in the poem felt when the meatball rolled onto the floor?"

Some possible student responses
a. He felt sad because he was hungry.
b. He was surprised because his sneeze knocked the meatball on the floor.
c. He was happy because he doesn't like meatballs.

Read number 3 with me. "Tell about a time when something you were eating fell on the floor. What did you do about it?" Have the students tell about their experiences with food falling on the floor.

Read number 4 with me. "What foods *really* grow on trees? What foods *don't* grow on trees?" Lead the class in a discussion about the sources of different foods.

Things to Do

Materials
- Page 34 in student book
- Drawing paper
- Crayons
- Writing paper
- Pencils

Look at the "Things to Do" on page 34 in your book. Ask each student to choose one of the three activities to do, or pick one for the whole class to do.

Let's read number 1 together. "Draw a picture of an imaginary tree that grows your favorite food. Draw three clues on the tree to help us guess what grows on your tree. See if the class can use the clues to guess your favorite food." Draw a picture of your food tree. On the tree, you might want to draw three ingredients that are in your favorite food. These could be the clues. Have the students draw pictures of trees that grow their favorite foods.

Let's read number 2 together. "Help cook some spaghetti for dinner. Sing 'On Top of Spaghetti' for your family." Ask the students to share this rhyme with their families the next time they prepare spaghetti.

Let's read number 3 together. "Write your own version of this poem. Here are some possible titles.
a. 'On Top of My Taco'
b. 'On Top of My Burger'
c. 'On Top of My Hot Dog'
Be sure to tell what rolls out of the door and what happens after that."

Copy one of the three titles on your paper. Then, write a new version of the poem about this food. Have the students write new versions of the poem.

Extending Language and Thinking

Activity

Objectives
- to identify words that go together
- to illustrate "go-togethers"

Materials
- Drawing paper and crayons

"Spaghetti and meatballs" make a good combination. There are many other things that go together, like shoes and socks, and hot dogs and buns. See if you can think of good "go-togethers" for these words.

pencils and _____
toothpaste and _____

Think of your own ideas for "go-togethers." Draw a picture of each object, and see if a friend can guess what it is. Have each student fold his paper in half and draw a picture on each half.

Strengthening Language for Second-Language Learners

Activity 1

Objectives
- to identify types of balls
- to identify characteristics of balls

Materials
- Chalkboard and chalk
- Drawing paper and crayons

"Meatballs" are an unusual kind of ball! There are many different types of balls that students can think of to add to a list. Ask the students to name the different types of balls they know. List the words on the chalkboard. The list might include football, basketball, snowball, soccer ball, rubber ball, etc. Concept development and vocabulary development can be encouraged as the students draw or add to the list while identifying such characteristics of balls as roundness, size, material, use in games, etc.

Activity 2

Objectives
- to promote understanding of compound words
- to practice forming compound words

Materials
- Chalkboard and chalk
- Circles of light brown construction paper
- Markers
- Scissors

The word *meatball* is a good example of two words joined to form a compound word. On the chalkboard, write *meatball*. Under *meatball,* list other familiar compounds such as *snowman, cowboy, bookcase, backyard,* etc. Then, ask the students to identify what these words have in common. Ask for suggestions of words to add to the list. Then, distribute circles of light brown construction paper. Have each student fold the circle in half. Tell the student to make a "compound meatball" using one of the words on the chalkboard. On each half of the meatball, have the student write one of the words that makes up the compound word. Then, have him cut the meatball on the fold.

The "meatballs" can be used for a practice activity in which students match up halves to form a compound word.

Reaching Across the Curriculum

Expanding Social Studies

Activity

Objective
- to discuss, compare, and taste pasta

Materials
- Different kinds of pasta

Spaghetti is a universal food staple. What kinds of noodles or pasta are familiar to your students? What have they eaten with spaghetti? Make a display of different kinds of pasta brought from home. This will lead to discussion, comparison, and good tasting.

Understanding Health Issues

Activity

Objective
- to discuss sneezing

Material
- None

Lead a class discussion about sneezes. **What causes us to sneeze? What happens when we sneeze? How can we prevent spreading germs to others when we sneeze?**

The powerful sneeze in "On Top of Spaghetti" can generate discussion about health reminders during rainy and wintry seasons.

Expanding Literature and Art

Activity 1

Objective
- to share a children's story

Material
- Children's book
  Hurwitz, Johanna. *Baseball Fever*. New York: Dell Publishing Company, Inc., 1983.

Baseball Fever by Johanna Hurwitz is an appealing story about a young baseball fan who has a misadventure with spaghetti and meatballs. You'll enjoy sharing this humorous book with your students!

Activity 2

Objective
- to create sequential pictures of the poem

Materials
- Drawing paper and crayons
- Tape

"Follow that Meatball!" pictures can outline the journey of the meatball in four sequential pictures from on the plate, to rolling out the door, then under a bush, and growing into a tree. Have a group of students draw one part for taping into the four-part sequence, or let each student produce all four stages. Final drawings can be used in subsequent presentations of the poem.

Lesson 12

Hey, Smarty . . . Zoo Party!

A pajama party featuring iguanas and armadillos should appeal to the vivid imaginations of students, especially when the house full of animals confronts unexpected parents!

Objectives:

Students will
- brainstorm a list of unusual animals.
- practice choral/oral reading.
- identify the natural habitat of selected animals.
- extend language and ideas through oral and written expression.

Warming Up for Reading

Materials
- Chalkboard and chalk

Write the following on the chalkboard.
Pajama party Friday night. Bring a pet!

You're about to get an invitation to an unusual sleep-over party, but there's a hitch! You have to bring a pet, and it can't be an ordinary pet. It has to be an *extraordinary* animal. What's the craziest animal you could possibly bring? Allow the students to work individually or in pairs to think up an "animal guest."

Okay, party time! Who's your guest? On the chalkboard, write the names of the animals suggested by the students.

Imagine what would happen if your folks came home and found the house invaded by this menagerie. That's exactly what happens in this poem about a pajama party for pets. Listen to see if any of our animals are a part of this Zoo Party.

Sharing the Poem

Materials
- Pages 35-36 in student book

Read the poem aloud to the students.

Hey, Smarty . . . Zoo Party!

Hey, smarty! Hey, smarty! I'm having a party.
Please come, but you must bring a pet.
Make it a weird one,
A strange but not feared one
That's never been seen by a vet.

I've got a soft pillow for an armadillo.
Chimpanzees are good for a laugh.
A hippo that's happy,
A croc that is snappy,
Or even a baby giraffe.

Hey, smarty! Hey, smarty! I'm having a party.
Please come, but you must bring a pet.
Make it a weird one,
A strange but not feared one
That's never been seen by a vet.

How about an iguana or even a llama?
There's room for a camel out back.
A bear that is cuddly,
A pig not too muddly,
Or even a three-legged yak.

Hey, smarty! Hey, smarty! I'm having a party.
Please come, but you must bring a pet.
Make it a weird one,
A strange but not feared one
That's never been seen by a vet.

(continued)

So bring your anteater. A penguin is neater.
A walrus will add to the fun.
There's a problem or two.
When my folks see our zoo,
You'd better be ready to run!

by Barbara Schmidt

**Did the poem mention any of our animals?
Were there any animals in the poem that
we didn't mention? What do you think your
parents would do if they found any of these
animals in the house?**

Pass out poem

~~Turn to page 35 in your book.~~ **Look at the
picture. Do you know what kind of animal
this is? Have you ever seen an animal like
this before? Look at the picture on page 36.
Is this animal more common than the one
we were just talking about? See if you can
find all the animal names in the poem.**
Students may need help with such animal names
as "armadillo," "yak," "llama," and "iguana."

**Let's read the poem aloud as if we were
giving the party and inviting a friend on
the telephone.** Demonstrate by holding an
imaginary telephone receiver to your ear as you
talk into an imaginary mouthpiece.

Divide the class into groups, and assign each
group one stanza to read. For subsequent
readings, assign one line to individual students.
The students should be reminded to keep the
poem moving and to use lots of expression.

Read the refrain altogether.

*Read it enough for kids to be
very familiar and*

Putting Ideas to Work

Things to Talk About

Materials
- Page 37 in student book
- Chalkboard and chalk

**Look at page 37 in your book. "Things to
Talk About" asks us to do some thinking
about the zoo party.**

**Read the first question with me. "What's
the most *unusual* animal at this party?"**
Write the students' responses on the chalkboard.

Some possible student responses — an
armadillo, an iguana, a yak

**Read the second question with me. "What
problems might be caused by having a
house party for these pets?" An unusual
party like this is bound to cause some
unusual problems. What problems might
occur if you invited all these animals to a
party at your house?**

Some possible student responses
a. I wouldn't know what kind of food to serve.
b. I might not be able to fit all the animals in
   the house.
c. The animals might make a mess.

**Read the third set of questions with me.
"Which of these animals might not get
along at a party? Why?" I bet that some of
these animals don't hang around together
very often! I wonder how a camel and a
penguin would get along? Tell us which of
the animals in the poem might not get
along. Why?**

Some possible student responses
a. a giraffe and a croc (They wouldn't be able to
   look at each other very easily.)
b. a camel and a penguin (The camel would
   probably want to be in a warm room, and the
   penguin would probably want to be in a cold
   room.)
c. a walrus and a croc (They might fight over
   who gets to sit in the bathtub.)

Things to Do

Materials
- Page 37 in student book
- Library sources
- Writing paper
- Pencils

Look at the "Things to Do" on page 37 in your book. Ask each student to choose one of the three activities to do, or pick one for the whole class to do. *Do all 3, Read them altogether first.*

Let's read number 1 together. "Choose an interesting animal that might make an unusual pet. Find out what your animal eats. Find out where it sleeps. Find out its habits. Write a mystery paragraph that gives clues about this animal but does not give away the animal's name. Read your paragraph to the class. See if the class can guess your animal from the clues you give." Have the students research and write about unusual animals. Then, have each student read her paragraph aloud. Let the other students try to guess the animal described in the paragraph. *Use wildlife encyclopedia's in bookcase by door.*

Let's read number 2 together. "Everybody likes a good party. If you were planning the best party ever, what would it be like? Write about it. Describe what would happen, what food you would serve, and when and where the party would take place. Share your ideas with the class. Vote on class favorites." This is your chance to plan your dream party! Pretend that anything is possible! Have the students write about imaginative parties. Then, have them share their ideas with the rest of the class.

Let's read number 3 together. "Draw several animals from the poem dressed for a pajama party." Encourage the students to use their own ideas and imaginations.

Pass out paper. Kids begin.

1/2 class uses encyclopedias (wildlife ones)

1/2 class does #2 and #3

Less Then switch.

Extending Language and Thinking

Activity 1

Objectives
- to create party invitations
- to plan a party

Materials
- Chalkboard and chalk
- Construction paper
- Pencils
- Crayons
- Bulletin board
- Writing paper

Now, it's our turn to have the party, and we get to do the inviting. What information will we need to include in the party invitation? On the chalkboard, write the following format for an invitation. Encourage the students to determine the date, time, and place of the party.

Date _____

Time _____

Place _____

Given by _____

Special Guest _____

Now, you get to make your own invitation. Be sure to put your name as host or hostess, and put in your own "special guest" animal. We'll share your invitations before we put them on the bulletin board. Provide the students with construction paper for making the invitations. Show them how to fold the paper to make it like a card. Have each student copy the format for the invitation on the inside of the card and design the front of the card.

If you were giving a party, what would your planning include? Encourage the students to consider refreshments, decorations, games, and prizes. Then, divide the students into groups to develop a "planning list" for each of these areas. This activity could lead to an actual class party celebrating a holiday or special event.

Activity 2

Objective
- to identify abbreviations

Materials
- Pages 35-36 in student book
- Chalkboard and chalk

This poem lends itself to a discussion of abbreviations. Have the students skim the poem to identify names that have been abbreviated ("vet," "hippo," and "croc"). On the chalkboard, write the abbreviations and spell out each name. Ask the students to suggest why the author of this poem abbreviated these names rather than spell them out. To illustrate the importance of using abbreviations in this poem, have the students reread the affected stanzas substituting complete words for abbreviations.

Since some abbreviations are commonly used in math, science, and social studies texts, guide the students in recognizing the importance of abbreviations. Ask the students to suggest commonly used abbreviations for each of the following categories:

Time: wk. — week, hr. — hour, mo. — month
Weights/Measurements:
  yd. — yard, lb. — pound, gal. — gallon,
  m — meter, kg — kilogram, l — liter
Title: Dr. — doctor, Mr. — mister,
  Mrs. — married woman, Ms. — married or
  unmarried woman
Places: IL — Illinois, MA — Massachusetts,
  CA — California

Strengthening Language for Second-Language Learners

Activity

Objective
- to identify animals through descriptions

Materials
- Chalkboard and chalk

On the chalkboard, write the names of some common animals such as *dog, cat, horse, cow, deer, bird,* and *fish.* Pronounce each word, and ask the students to repeat its pronunciation as you point to the word.

Read the following descriptions aloud, and ask the students to identify the animal that matches each description.

1. **This animal has four feet and lives in the forest.**
2. **This animal builds nests and lives in trees.**
3. **This animal lives in the ocean, in rivers, and in lakes.**
4. **This animal barks and often chases cats.**
5. **This animal has four feet and is fun to ride.**
6. **This animal has four paws, a tail, and says "meow."**

Reaching Across the Curriculum
Developing Creative Expression

Activity

Objectives
- to create a new stanza for the poem
- to write an article about the animals invited to the party

Materials
- Writing paper
- Pencils

Using the following poem pattern, ask the students to fill in the animals they want to invite.

Hey, smarty! Hey, smarty! I'm having a party.
Please come, but you must bring a pet.
Make it a weird one,
A strange but not feared one
That's never been seen by a vet.

I've got _____ _____ _____ _____ for
a(n) _____ .
_____ are good for a laugh.
A _____ that's happy,
A _____ that is snappy,
Or even a baby giraffe.

Ask each student to write a newspaper article or television newscast describing what happened when the guest showed up with the different animals mentioned in the poem. Have each student present her news article to the class.

Exploring Science and Social Studies

Activity

Objective
- to locate and share information about the animals in the poem

Materials
- Chalkboard and chalk
- Library sources
- Writing paper
- Pencils

Ask the students to locate the name of each animal listed in the poem. On the chalkboard, write the following animal names: *armadillo, chimpanzee, hippo, croc, giraffe, iguana, llama, camel, bear, pig, yak, anteater, penguin,* and *walrus*. Divide the class into groups, assigning each group one or two animals from the list. Do not include the bear or the pig because they are common to many continents. Have each group use a science text, a social science text, or an encyclopedia to locate

1. the continent(s) where each animal is found.
2. two interesting facts about the animal to share with the class.

Extending through Art

Activity 1

Objectives
- to create animal pictures
- to locate where animals live on a world map

Materials
- Drawing paper
- Crayons
- Bulletin board
- World map
- Tacks
- Yarn

Ask the students to draw pictures of the animals they've researched. Pictures may be posted on a bulletin board along with a world map. Using pieces of yarn, have the students connect each animal to its "home continent" on the world map.

Activity 2

Objective
- to create "stuffed" animals

Materials
- Large pieces of heavy paper
- Pencils
- Paint and paintbrushes
- Crayons
- Glue or stapler
- Shredded newspaper

Using large pieces of heavy paper, have each student draw a large outline of her animal and cut it out. Have the student trace her outline on heavy paper and cut it out. This will give her two outlines, one for each side of her animal. After painting or coloring the sides, glue or staple the edges together. Leave an opening to stuff the animal with shredded newspaper. Glue or staple the opening shut. These stuffed animals can make a colorful class zoo.

Do I Hafta?

To your young students, life probably seems to be filled with "gottas" and "oughtas." That's why you'll enjoy empathizing with the children in this bouncy poem.

Objectives:

Students will

- relate personal experiences to poem content.
- practice choral/oral reading.
- evaluate the fairness of demands.
- engage in creative word play.
- extend language and ideas through oral and written expression.

Warming Up for Reading

Material

- None   *Ring the Bell on my desk*

After capturing the student's attention by blowing a whistle or pounding your fist on your desk, say the following in a commanding and authoritarian voice. **Now, hear this! I want the talking stopped, the desks cleaned, and everyone sitting up straight** *immediately!* **I want five pages of math homework turned in tomorrow morning with** *no* **grumbling and** *no* **excuses!**

Pause for a moment and say the following in a calmer voice. **Now, how does it feel to hear a whole bunch of orders like that? When I was your age, I got tired of being told to do this and to do that all the time, too. And from the sound of this poem, things haven't changed much. See if any of the children in this poem remind you of yourself in any way.**

say "Does your teacher even say this?" So that won't sound like the mean sub!

Sharing the Poem

Materials

- Pages 38-39 in student book
- Chalkboard and chalk

Read the poem aloud in an exasperated voice encouraging the students to chime in on the chorus.

Do I Hafta?

Hey, Tonio Balonio,
You **gotta** get off the phonio!

Hey, Julio Padoolio,
You **gotta** get dressed for schoolio!

Hey, Lydio, you kiddio,
You **gotta** stop watching video!

Gotta do thisios; Gotta do thatios.
Gotta and oughta are driving me batios!

Hey, Rosio O'Gradio,
You **gotta** turn down your radio!

Hey, Junio, get a broomio.
You **gotta** clean up your roomio!

Hey, Sunnio, you funnio,
You **gotta** stop spending monio!

Gotta do thisios; Gotta do thatios.
Gotta and oughta are driving me batios!

Hey, Kittio, don't quittio.
You **gotta** go baby sittio!

Hey, Flashio, don't dashio,
You **gotta** take out the trashio!

(continued)

Hey, Cathio McGraffio,
You **gotta** take a bathio,
And don't forget your mathio,
And don't just grin and laughio!

Gotta do thisios; Gotta do thatios.
Gotta and oughta are driving me batios!

 by Barbara Schmidt

Did you hear anything in the poem that sounds familiar? Who do you think is doing the talking? Who's saying the chorus?

Pass out poem

Turn to page 38 in your book. Look at the pictures on pages 38 and 39. What are the children doing? How do they look? Let's read the poem aloud together. Encourage the students to read aloud with lots of expression.

What does the poet do with names and words to make the poem bounce along? Could you do that to your name? On the chalkboard, list some of the students' "new" names with "io" added to the end of each name.

Now, let's read the poem aloud again. How will your voices sound when you give the commands? How will your voices sound when you read the chorus? Let's get out a lot of frustration when we read the chorus! Lead the students in an expressive reading of the poem. Then, assign individual stanzas to various students while the whole class reads the chorus.

Insist on hand raising and no calling out!

Putting Ideas to Work

Things to Talk About

Materials
- Page 40 in student book
- Chalkboard and chalk

Look at page 40 in your book. "Things to Talk About" asks us to do some thinking about "gottas."

Read number 1 with me. "Which of the 'gottas' in this poem remind you of things you hear at home?" List the students' responses on the chalkboard.

Some possible student responses
a. Get off the phone!
b. Clean up your room!
c. Take out the trash!

Read number 2 with me. "Which 'gotta' do you get the most tired of hearing? Why?"

Some possible student responses
a. Turn down your radio. I don't think it's too loud.
b. Get off the phone. I have important things to talk about.
c. Take a bath. I don't think I'm dirty.

Read number 3 with me. "Are children the only ones who have 'gottas'? What are some demands that grown-ups have?" Sometimes children think they're the only ones who have "gottas," but grown-ups have them, too. What are some "gottas" that grown-ups have as demands?

Some possible student responses
a. Grown-ups have to cook meals.
b. Grown-ups have to pay bills.
c. Grown-ups have to drive children places.

Read number 4 with me. "What's the difference between 'gottas' that are *fair* and 'gottas' that are *unfair?* Give an example of each." Discuss the difference between *fair* and *unfair* demands. Then, ask the students to suggest examples of each.

Some possible student responses
fair — Make your bed.
unfair — Pick up your sister's dirty clothes.

Lesson 13   **67**

Can do capitalization lesson on next page

Things to Do

Materials

- Page 40 in student book
- Writing paper
- Pencils

Look at the "Things to Do" on page 40 in your book. Ask each student to choose one of three activities to do, or pick one for the whole class to do. *Kids do #1 and #2*

Let's read number 1 together. "Think of some 'gottas' to add to the ones in the poem. Continue the 'Do I Hafta?' poem by adding your own personal list." Have the students write down their ideas.

Let's read number 2 together. "Fold a piece of paper in half the long way. At the top of one half, write Fair Requests. At the top of the other half, write Unfair Requests. Put requests from the poem and from your own personal list under the appropriate title." When the students have finished, let them share their papers with the rest of the class.

Let's read number 3 together. "Create a rhyme using the poet's technique of adding 'io' to names and words." Have the students create new versions of the poem.

Extending Language and Thinking

Activity 1

Objectives

- to discuss the usage of slang expressions
- to create a slang dictionary

Materials

- Chalkboard and chalk
- Chart paper
- Strips of colored construction paper
- Markers
- Tape

Why does the poet use expressions like "hey," "hafta," "gotta," and "oughta"? How could you change the words in the poem so they sound like correct language? Does that change the feeling of the poem at all?

Some poets use slang expressions like "hey" to create a mood. Do you use slang? What are some common slang expressions that you have used or heard? List the students' responses on the chalkboard.

Our language is constantly growing and changing. You will find words in a new dictionary that weren't there before. Some words were once slang expressions and weren't considered to be good usage, but then they became acceptable because of popular usage. Maybe some of the expressions on the chalkboard appear in a dictionary or will appear someday. We're going to get a head start on the publishers by creating our own slang dictionary. Slang is colorful, and we want our dictionary to reflect that feeling.

Post a large piece of chart paper on the wall. Divide the class into groups. Make each group responsible for coming up with at least ten common slang expressions and their meanings. Have them write their expressions and definitions on strips of colored construction paper, which will be taped to the chart paper on the wall.

Caution the students to use expressions that are suitable for display. Ask each group to share their contributions before taping the colorful strips to the wall. Encourage the class to discuss all the expressions and their meanings. If there is disagreement or if a meaning isn't clear, explain to the students that dictionaries provide multiple meanings for some words. Therefore, the slang dictionary can have several definitions beside each expression.

Activity 2

Objectives
- to discuss the literal and figurative meanings of expressions
- to illustrate literal and figurative meanings

Materials
- Chalkboard and chalk
- Drawing paper
- Pencils
- Crayons

What does "driving me bats" mean? What other expressions could you use to show that something is really beginning to bother you? On the chalkboard, write the expressions offered by the students.

Expressions like "stop bugging me" and "you're driving me up a wall" are kinds of figurative language. These expressions paint very vivid images in our minds. These expressions have double meanings, and that can be confusing and even funny to readers. If you had never heard the expression "driving me bats," what picture might you get in your mind?

Write down a common expression that could have two very different meanings, a literal meaning for someone who has never heard it before and a figurative meaning. Then, draw two pictures. One should illustrate the literal meaning and the other should illustrate the figurative meaning.

Strengthening Language for Second-Language Learners

Activity

Objective
- to reinforce basic language skills

Materials
- Chalkboard and chalk
- Pages 38-39 in student book

Use any of the following with the poem to reinforce basic language skills.

Capitalization — Identify and list on the chalkboard the names in the poem. Discuss the fact that proper names begin with capital letters.

Poetic style — Point out that some of the words in the poem are in bold-faced type. Explain that this is done to show greater emphasis.

Word patterns — Use the poem to identify and discuss rhyming word patterns and to generate a list of additional rhyming words.

Slang expressions — Discuss the expression "hey." **When and how is it used? What does it mean? What other common expressions do you freqently hear?**

Reaching Across the Curriculum

Developing Creative Expression

Activity

Objectives
- to create a standard English version of the poem
- to conduct a survey to compare versions

Materials
- Writing paper
- Pencils

Translate the poem into standard English eliminating the slang expressions like "hey" and "gotta." Then, conduct a survey. Give both versions of the poem to someone who has never read it before. Ask him which version he likes better. Have him tell you why. Share the results of your survey with the class.

Expanding Social Studies

Activity

Objective
- to have a family discussion on "gottas"

Material
- None

Involve your family in a discussion of some of the "gottas" that bug them. Ask your parents what requests they remember getting annoyed about when they were your age. Discuss the feelings that are brought about by constant demands. Discuss why you think certain demands are fair and certain demands are unfair. Discuss how to avoid getting nagged over and over again to do certain things. Share the results of your discussion with the class.

Expanding Literature

Activity

Objective
- to share children's books

Materials
- Children's books
  Gwynne, Fred. *The King Who Rained.* New York: Julian Messner, 1981.
  Gwynne, Fred. *A Chocolate Moose for Dinner.* New York: Julian Messner, 1981.
- Pencils
- Drawing paper
- Crayons

Share Fred Gwynne's *The King Who Rained* and/or *A Chocolate Moose for Dinner.* Both books are filled with humorous illustrations depicting literal interpretations of figurative language. After sharing Gwynne's figurative language and illustrations, encourage the students to suggest common expressions that can be taken literally. Have the students write their expressions on drawing paper. Below the expressions, have the students draw illustrations that literally depict the expressions.

Lesson 14

Loquacious Lucy Longbreath

"Loquacious Lucy Longbreath" will introduce your class to a young lady whose incessant chatter is driving her friends crazy. Challenge your students to think of a more satisfactory way to make Lucy quiet down than the solution suggested in the poem.

Objectives:

Students will
- understand the meaning of "loquacious."
- practice choral/oral reading.
- relate personal experiences to content.
- extend language and ideas through oral and written expression.

Warming Up for Reading

Materials
- Chalkboard and chalk

On the chalkboard, write *Who do you know that is so "loquacious" that he or she talks constantly?*

You must know someone who fits the description on the chalkboard. Have you figured out what the word *loquacious* means?

Loquacious **means "very talkative or wordy." What's a slang expression that means the same as a "loquacious" person?** Students may respond with bigmouth, loudmouth, chatterbox, motor-mouth, etc.

Sometimes talking too much creates problems. If your name is Loquacious Lucy Longbreath, you may be headed for trouble! Listen to this poem, and decide if you would want to spend time with Lucy.

Sharing the Poem

Material
- Page 41 in student book

Read the poem expressively to the students.

Loquacious Lucy Longbreath

Lucy Longbreath is a talker,
    And it's no laughing matter.
She's driving everybody nuts
    With her constant chatter.

She jabbers while she's shopping
    And all day long at school.
She jabbers at the movies
    And in the swimming pool.

Jabber, jabber, jabber.
    Oh, you loquacious child!
Jabber, jabber, jabber.
    You're driving us all wild!

She jabbers in the morning.
    She jabbers all day through.
And even when she goes to bed,
    Her mouth is moving, too!

She jabbers to her teachers.
    Her tongue is never still.
They're taking a collection
    To buy a **shut-up** pill.

Lucy! Lucy! Lucy!
    You really are a pain!
Your prattle, prattle, prattle,
    Is driving us **insane**!

by Maurice Poe

Whew! See what I mean about loquacious? How do the people in the poem react to Lucy? How does Lucy's name fit her?

Turn to page 41 in your book and you'll get to meet her personally. Look at the picture of Lucy. What is she doing? How do you think people react to her? Find the parts of the poem where words are repeated. What are those words?

When we get to those parts, make your voice get louder each time you repeat the word. Let's try it together using lots of expression. Chorally chant the poem several times. Then, each stanza can be read by individual students with the whole class joining in on the parts where the words "jabber," "Lucy," and "prattle" are repeated.

Putting Ideas to Work

Things to Talk About

Material
- Page 42 in student book

Look at page 42 in your book. "Things to Talk About" tells us to do some thinking about Lucy.

Read the first question with me. "Why do you think Lucy is so loquacious?" Why do you suppose Lucy talks so much?

Some possible student responses
a. She's a nervous person.
b. She thinks she has important things to say.
c. She likes the sound of her own voice.

Read the second question with me. "How do the people in the poem feel about Lucy's behavior?"

Possible student response — It's driving them wild and insane.

Read the third set of questions with me. "How do the people plan to solve Lucy's problem? Do you think that's a good solution? Why? Why not?" Discuss with the students how people are "taking a collection to buy a **shut-up** pill." Then, ask them whether or not they think this is a good idea and why.

Some possible student responses
a. Yes, that may be the only way to shut Lucy up.
b. No, people should be more understanding and try to help Lucy with her problem.

Read the fourth question with me. "Do you know anyone who reminds you of Lucy?" Have the students tell who reminds them of Lucy.

Things to Do

Materials
- Page 42 in student book
- Writing paper
- Pencils
- Chart paper
- Marker

Look at the "Things to Do" on page 42 in your book. Ask each student to choose one of the three activities to do, or pick one for the whole class to do.

Let's read number 1 together. "Make a list of all the words in the poem that mean *talkative*. Then, add words not in the poem to your list. Combine your words and those of other students to make a class list of words that mean the same as *talkative*." Have the students write lists of synonyms for *talkative*. Then, compile the students' lists onto a chart.

Let's read number 2 together. "Write about a time when talking too much got you into trouble. Where were you? Who were you talking to? Why did you get into trouble? How did you feel?" Have the students write about times where talking got them into trouble.

Let's read number 3 together. "Fold a piece of paper in half the long way. At the top of one half, write Times to Talk. At the top of the other half, write Times *Not* to Talk. Under each title, list appropriate times. Share your list with the class." Have the students list Times to Talk and Times *Not* to Talk.

Extending Language and Thinking

Activity

Objective
- to engage in problem solving

Materials
- Chalkboard and chalk
- Writing paper
- Pencils

What did you think about the "solution" at the end of the poem? We may be able to come up with a better way of getting Lucy to quiet down, but we need to act fast before she loses all her friends. I think she needs some professional advice. Have you ever heard of any famous people who give advice when someone writes to them with a problem? On the chalkboard, write a list of the people that the students name.

Today you're going to write to "Dear Blabby" describing Lucy Longbreath's problem and asking for help. Be sure to explain why Lucy's constant talking is causing a problem. Be tactful. Don't write things that are going to hurt someone's feelings!

After you finish your letter requesting advice, pass it to your neighbor. Your neighbor will then write an answering letter on the back of your request. The answering letter must offer a practical solution to Lucy's problem. We'll share your letters and decide which solutions make the most sense.

Strengthening Language for Second-Language Learners

Activity

Objective
- to discuss the difficulty in practicing a new language

Material
- None

Students who are developing a language other than their first language are often hesitant to practice the new language in social situations. A sensitive discussion on the vulnerability of using an unfamiliar language can be a worthwhile experience.

Practicing a new language involves risks, just like practicing any new ability. How does it feel to have someone laugh at your mistakes? What encourages you to practice harder? How could you help someone who is learning a new language? What is frustrating about learning a new language?

Reaching Across the Curriculum

Developing Creative Expression

Activity 1

Objective
- to discuss and write about thoughtless comments

Materials
- Writing paper
- Pencils

Everyone has experienced a time when they said something they later regretted. This experience could prove to be a worthwhile topic for discussion and creative writing. **Was there ever a time when you spoke without thinking and were sorry for what you said? Write about what happened.**

Activity 2

Objective
- to write about the advantages and disadvantages of talking

Materials
- Writing paper
- Pencils

Talking is a wonderful and useful way to communicate, but sometimes it gets people into trouble. Write about some advantages and disadvantages of talking. What problems would we have if we weren't able to speak? What problems can speaking create?

Expanding Social Studies

Activity

Objective
- to discuss forms of nonverbal communication

Materials
- Chalkboard and chalk

Ask the students to think of ways to communicate other than talking. **How could you send a message to someone without talking?** Help the students become aware that we can communicate nonverbally through writing, codes, computers, telegraphs, body language, etc. Further explain that people can express how they feel through art, music, dance, dramatization, etc. On the chalkboard, write all the nonverbal forms of communication you discuss.

Discuss with the students what it would be like to live in a world with no communication. **What would it be like to live in a world where people could not communicate with one another? Can you think of advantages? Can you think of problems that would arise?**

Exploring Science

Activity

Objective
- to discuss communication within the animal world

Materials
- Library sources

Are humans the only animals that communicate by using spoken sounds? Lead a discussion on how various members of the animal world communicate. This discussion could lead the students into a research project on animal behavior.

Lesson 15

Strange Names

You and your students are about to meet some people with intriguing names. For starters, there's Anna Septic, a nurse; Clara Net, a music teacher; and Cal Q. Late, a math teacher. Your students will chuckle as they tongue-trip through this lighthearted play on names.

Objectives:

Students will
- infer relationships.
- practice choral/oral reading.
- identify occupational attributes.
- create names for people that correlate with occupations or behaviors.
- extend language and ideas through oral and written expression.

Warming Up for Reading

Materials
- Chalkboard and chalk

On the chalkboard, write *What's My Line?*

Today we have some guests coming to our classroom. Before we meet these people, we're going to play a game called "What's My Line?" I'll write the names of some of our guests on the chalkboard. Using only the person's name, try to figure out what that person might do for a living. Write the following names on the chalkboard one at a time, and let the students guess what each person might do for a living.

Jill E. Bean (candy taster, candy maker, candy store owner)
Bill D. Homes (house builder, carpenter, construction worker)
Ann E. Malkeeper (veterinarian, zoo keeper)

Today's poem features more characters with unusual names. As I read the poem aloud, listen to how each person's name relates to what that person does.

Sharing the Poem

Materials
- Chalkboard and chalk
- Pages 43-45 in student book

Read the poem in a lighthearted manner encouraging the students to join in on the chorus.

Strange Names

**There is a town in Old Kentucky
    where the people have strange names,
And it's hard to find a Jeffrey
    or a Jennie or a James.**

For example,

Anna Septic
    is a nurse,
And Mack Aronie
    is a cook.
Clara Net's
    the music teacher.
Robin Banks works
    as a crook.

Torrey Teller
    is a gossip.
Cal Q. Late —
    he teaches math.
Penny Pincher
    is a banker.
I. M. Durrty
    needs a bath!

(continued)

Tiny Totters
    owns a preschool.
Lotta Porkker
    raises hogs.
Ms. Adventures
    likes to travel.
Ima Barker
    raises dogs.

There is a town in old Kentucky
    where the people have strange names,
And it's hard to find a Jeffrey
    or a Jennie or a James.

For example,

Ray Darr
    is a traffic cop.
Etta Lott
    is overweight.
Gar Beige
    picks up trash and rubbish.
Al Alone's
    without a mate.

Bea Strickenstern's
    a principal.
Rita Book
    reads all the time.
Jackie Rabbit
    is a runner.
Tuffy Kopp's
    in charge of crime.

Terri Cloth's
    a good dressmaker.
April Full
    is quite a prankster.
Patty Cake
    is the town baker.
Jewel Theaf,
    well, he's a gangster.

There is a town in old Kentucky
    where the people have strange names,
And it's hard to find a Jeffrey
    or a Jennie or a James.

                by Maurice Poe

Why do you think "Strange Names" is a good title for this poem? What was the name of the nurse? How does her name fit her job? What was the cook's name? How does his name fit his job? What does Clara Net do? How does her name fit? What other names do you remember, and what do those names tell you about the people? On the chalkboard, list the names and occupations or behaviors.

Turn to page 43 in your book. Look at the picture. What is the man doing? See if you can find his name in the poem. Now, turn to page 44 and look at the pictures on pages 44 and 45. Can you figure out who these people are? Find their names in the poem. Let's read the poem aloud together. Be sure that your tongue doesn't get in the way as we read. Lead the class in a group reading of the poem.

Divide the class into six groups. Lead the class in a group reading with each group reading one stanza and everybody reading the chorus.

For subsequent readings, assign individual students characters in the poem. There are twenty-four. Ask each student to think of an appropriate thing that his character might say. For example, Anna Septic might say, "Hold still while I put a bandage on that cut." Then, have the class read the poem aloud, stopping after each character is named to allow the student to say his expression. The students might think up something similar to the following.

Class: **"Anna Septic is a nurse,"**
Student: **"Hold still while I put a bandage on that cut."**
Class: **"And Mack Aronie is a cook."**
Student: **"Bacon and eggs coming up!"**

Putting Ideas to Work

Things to Talk About

Material
• Page 46 in student book

Look at page 46 in your book. "Things to Talk About" asks us to do some thinking about the people in "Strange Names."

Read the first question with me. "How do these names fit the people?" Do the people's names tell anything about them? What?

Possible student response — Each person's name tells something about what that person does.

Read the second question with me. "Whose name do you think is the most unusual?"

Some possible student responses — Mack Aronie, Robin Banks, Patty Cake

Read the third question with me. "Which of the names is your favorite?"

Some possible student responses — I. M. Durrty, Gar Beige, Terri Cloth

Read the fourth set of questions with me. "If you could be one of the people in the poem, which one would you be? Why?"

Some possible student responses
a. Ima Barker — I'd love to raise dogs.
b. Bea Strickenstern — I could run this school.
c. April Full — I like to play jokes on people.

Things to Do

Materials
- Page 46 in student book
- Writing paper
- Pencils

Look at the "Things to Do" on page 46 in your book. Ask each student to choose one of three activities to do, or pick one for the whole class to do.

Let's read number 1 together. "Copy the following names on your paper. Beside each name, write what each person might do for a living." Let's read the names together. They are "Ida Liver," "Janet Torr," "Clay Potts," "Morris Code," and "Leah Tard." Can you think of a job or behavior that fits each name? Have the

students copy these names and write what each person might do for a living or hobby.

Let's read number 2 together. "Make up some of your own names. Write them on your paper. Beside each name, tell how the name matches what the person does or how the person acts." After the students have had time to make up some new names, have them share the names with the rest of the class.

Let's read number 3 together. "Make up a story about what happens when two of the people in the poem get married. Tell about what their lives are like, how many children they have, what the names of the children are, and if the children are like the parents." Have the students write stories about the marriage of two people from the poem.

Extending Language and Thinking

Activity 1

Objective
- to identify occupations from names

Materials
- Chalkboard and chalk

On the chalkboard, write the following list of names. Do not write the occupations.

Ann Athlete	(gym teacher)
Barbie Kew	(cook)
Will Travel	(travel agent)
Dan D. Lyons	(gardener)
Lotta Dough	(banker, millionaire)
Carol Songs	(singer)
Jim Lokkers	(gym teacher)
Moe DeLaun	(gardener)
Renee Day	(weather forecaster)
U. R. Sic	(doctor, nurse)

Read through the list with the students. Then, break the class into small groups to brainstorm possible occupations for each name listed. Call upon groups to share their responses. Write the responses beside the appropriate names.

Activity 2

Objective
- to create names to match occupations

Materials
- Chalkboard and chalk

Have the students brainstorm a list of various occupations. Write their suggestions on the chalkboard. Then, challenge the students to make up names that match or describe a person for each of the occupations listed.

Strengthening Language for Second-Language Learners

Activity

Objective
- to discuss future occupations

Materials
- Chalkboard and chalk

What kind of job would you like to have when you finish school? Write the following sentence frame on the chalkboard.

I would like to be a(n) _____ ,
because _____ .

Model for the students how to use the sentence frame to tell what job they would like to have eventually. (For example, *I would like to be a carpenter, because I like to build things with my hands.*) Have the students take turns using this sentence frame to tell what they would like to do and why.

Reaching Across the Curriculum

Expanding Social Studies

Activity 1

Objective
- to discuss the origin of last names

Materials
- Chalkboard and chalk

What would life be like if you were called by a number instead of by a name? Can you imagine being called 5-3-3-2-1-2-6-4-4?

Fortunately, we have names, which are far more personal than numbers. Most of us have at least two names, a first name and a last name. This was not always the case. Long ago, people were given only first names such as *William.* When William married and had a son named William, things got confusing. When someone called William's name, were they calling William the father or William the son? To solve the problem, William the son became known as Williamson. Have the students suggest other last names that end in *son.* Write these names on the chalkboard.

Last names often described what a person did for a living. A person named Forest may have lived in a forest or may have cut trees for a living. On the chalkboard, write the names *Shepherd* and *Taylor.* Ask the students to think of occupations that might have led to these names. Have the students think of other common last names that describe what the person might have done for a living. (For example, *Baker, Smith, Cook, Farmer,* and *Wood.*) Write the names on the chalkboard.

Activity 2

Objectives
- to identify the meanings of first names
- to write descriptive paragraphs about name meanings

Materials
- Library sources
- Writing paper
- Pencils

Most proper names have definite meanings. For example, Vanessa means "butterfly," Irene means "peace," and William means "strong protector." Have each student interview his parents to discover how his first name was chosen. As a research project, have the students go to the library to find a book on the meaning of names. Tell each student to write a descriptive paragraph about how his first name was selected and what it means.

Exploring Geography

Activity 1

Objectives
- to match names and states
- to invent names to match states

Materials
- Chalkboard and chalk
- Map of the United States
- Writing paper
- Pencils

On the chalkboard, write some or all of the following names. (Do not write the names of the states.)

Mrs. Ippi	(Mississippi)
Ida Hoe	(Idaho)
Calli Forna	(California)
Y. O. Ming	(Wyoming)
Mitch I. Gan	(Michigan)
Connie T. Cutt	(Connecticut)
Monty Anna	(Montana)

Display a map of the United States, and ask the students to figure out which states the names match. Write the names of the states next to the names of people. Then, ask the students to make up names for people similar to those on the chalkboard. Tell each student to write at least one name on a sheet of paper. Have the students consult a map of the United States to make sure that each name matches the name of a state. Once the students have come up with some names, play "Guess My State." Call upon a student to write a person's name on the chalkboard. That student should then pick another member of the class to identify the state suggested by the name. The student who is guessing does so by going to the map of the United States, pointing to the state, and saying its name. If the student called upon is correct, he writes a name on the chalkboard and calls upon another student to come to the map and identify the state. The game continues until all students have had an opportunity to participate.

Activity 2

Objective
- to invent names to match cities

Material
- Map of a state

Have the students study their own state by selecting various cities within their state and formulating people's names to match the names of the cities. The following are examples of some people's names that match names of cities.

Hugh Stone	(Houston)
C. Attle	(Seattle)
Al Banny	(Albany)

Activity 3

Objectives
- to research individual states
- to illustrate state flags

Materials
- Library sources
- Writing paper
- Pencils
- Drawing paper
- Crayons

Studying the states of the United States can be interesting and fun. Divide the class into groups, and assign each group a number of states. Each group is to do research on the origin and meaning of state names. Have each group find the state slogan or motto, the state flower, and state animal.

Have the students draw pictures of their state flag, and tell them to write information from their research beneath the pictures.

Lesson 16

Instant Indigestion

Burgers with whipped cream? The wild food combinations in this humorous selection will whet any young student's appetite and encourage creative juices!

Objectives:

Students will
- contribute personal choices during discussion.
- visualize descriptive language.
- practice choral/oral reading.
- complete a patterned rhyme.
- use descriptive adjectives.
- extend language and ideas through oral and written expression.

Warming Up for Reading

Materials
- Chalkboard and chalk

On the chalkboard, write the following:
TODAY'S MENU
Mustard Milkshake
Hot Dog with Peanut Butter
Squash Seeds on Watermelon

Something's gone haywire in our cafeteria! What do you think about TODAY'S MENU? Does it sound appetizing? Can you think of a crazy food combination? Accept the students' ideas, and list them on the chalkboard.

If you think *these* were unusual, wait until you hear what the people in our poem ate. Close your eyes and see if you can picture these foods without getting indigestion. I'll be asking you which was your favorite, so listen carefully!

Sharing the Poem

Materials
- Pages 47-48 in student book

Read the poem aloud to the students.

Instant Indigestion

There was a young boy
   from Blue Moon Lake
Who sprinkled ketchup
   on his cake.

Would you believe
   that down in Rye
They're putting fish
   on pizza pie?

A teacher I heard of
   likes to eat
Spaghetti with squash seeds
   for a treat.

And how 'bout the girl
   from Waterloo
Who mashes peanuts
   in her stew?

Burgers with whipped cream,
   tacos and jelly,
Sound like an awful
   pain in the belly!

There were some students
   in East Malone.
If you want a last line,
   write your own!

by Barbara Schmidt and Maurice Poe

Which food combination sounded good to you? Ask the students to contribute their favorites.

Now it's your turn. Turn to page 47 in your book. Look at the picture. What is the girl eating? Look at the picture on page 48. What is the boy about to eat? Do either of these food combinations sound good to you?

Imagine that you are a reporter on an evening news program telling about strange food happenings. As we take turns reading each stanza of the poem, try to use a very serious voice and expression. You may want to demonstrate by reading a couple of stanzas. Then, divide the poem into sections, assigning each section to a student. Have the students read the poem several times so that everyone has an opportunity to share a stanza.

In the last stanza, we're told to write our own last line. What word will the last word of our new line have to rhyme with? What are some food words that rhyme with Malone? Let's see if we can write an ending to the poem using "ice cream cone" to rhyme with "Malone." The students may think up an ending similar to the following.

There were some students
in East Malone
Who ate cooked beets
in an ice cream cone.

After the students agree on a new ending, ask them to add some pizzazz to the poem by substituting new descriptive words. Have the students think of new words to use in place of "young" in the first stanza. Some possibilities are "weird," "odd," and "strange." Remind the students that the replacement word must contain the same number of syllables as the original word. Have them replace other descriptive words in the poem. Duplicate the students' revised version of the poem for rereading, for illustrating, and for display.

Putting Ideas to Work

Things to Talk About

Materials
- Page 49 in student book
- Chalkboard and chalk

Look at page 49 in your book. "Things to Talk About" asks us to do some thinking about food.

Read number 1 with me. "Why do you think this poem is called 'Instant Indigestion'?"

Some possible student responses
a. I'd get a bellyache eating all that stuff.
b. Just hearing about the foods makes me sick.
c. Those foods would taste terrible.

Read number 2 with me. "How would you get someone to try a new food they had never tasted?"

Some possible student responses
a. I would tell her that it tastes delicious.
b. I would tell her that it would make her big and strong.
c. I would tell her that she would only have to try one small bite.

Read number 3 with me. "Has there ever been a time when you ate something that gave you 'an awful pain in the belly'? Tell about it." I remember one time when I ate . . . Share a personal experience or make one up. Then, have the students share personal experiences.

Some possible student responses
a. I ate too much Thanksgiving dinner.
b. I ate a giant bucket of popcorn at the movies.
c. I ate a large pizza.

Read number 4 with me. "What is the weirdest food you have ever heard of anyone eating?" Some people like to eat things that sound pretty weird to me, like frogs' legs. How about you? What's the weirdest food you've ever heard of someone eating? List the students' responses on the chalkboard.

Some possible student responses
a. a chocolate-covered ant
b. a peanut butter and celery sandwich
c. scrambled eggs and ketchup

Read number 5 with me. "People have very different likes and dislikes about food. How would you convince a friend not to make fun of another person's choice?"

Some possible student responses
a. I'd tell her that if she tried the food, she might like it, too.
b. I'd tell her that it's not nice to make fun of people's choices.
c. I'd tell her that her choice might seem funny to someone else.

Things to Do

Materials
- Page 49 in student book
- Writing paper
- Pencils

Look at the "Things to Do" on page 49 in your book. Ask each student to choose one of the three activities to do, or pick one for the whole class to do.

Let's read number 1 together. "Create your own new and unusual ice cream flavors using words that begin with the same first letter. Some examples might be *Luscious Lizard Licorice* or *Spinach Supreme*." Use your imagination and try to use more than one descriptive word for each flavor. Have the students write down the names of their new ice cream flavors. Then, have them share their lists with the rest of the class.

Let's read number 2 together. "Make a list of your five favorite foods and a list of five foods you dislike. Compare your lists with a friend's." Have the students create two food lists. Then, divide the class into pairs for discussion.

Let's read number 3 together. "Make up a menu for a totally incredible breakfast including all of your favorite foods. Use mouth-watering descriptions." Have the students create unique, descriptive breakfast menus.

Extending Language and Thinking

Activity 1

Objective
- to create unusual menus of favorite foods

Materials
- Writing paper
- Pencils

Have the class brainstorm a list of favorite food words. Have each student offer at least one food word. Tell the students to list each word on paper. Then, have the students work in groups to make up menus that offer the strangest combinations of these favorite foods. After sharing these combinations with the whole class, let the students vote on "Room _____'s Weirdest Menu."

Activity 2

Objective
- to classify and categorize food words

Materials
- List of food favorites from **Activity 1**
- Index cards
- Markers

The list of food favorites from Activity 1 can become the basis for classifying and categorizing food words. Ask the students to see if any of the words on the list have something in common. **What do they have in common? What name could be given to this group of words? Could they be called Foods We Eat with Our Fingers, Foods We Eat Raw, or Desserts?** Encourage the students to work in pairs or teams to come up with several ways of categorizing the list of food favorites. Have the students write each category on an index card listing all the foods that go with that category. Keep the index cards together for on-going independent activities.

Strengthening Language for Second-Language Learners

Activity 1

Objective
- to discuss foods of different cultures

Materials
- Drawing paper
- Crayons
- Markers
- Bulletin board

The topic of food is a natural for language development. Every culture has unique dishes, although similarities exist that cross cultures. Encourage the students to draw pictures of some of these food favorites, label the pictures, and display them on a "Food Around the World" bulletin board. A comparative discussion of various kinds of bread, noodles, desserts, and drinks can take place.

Activity 2

Objective
- to create a "Food Dictionary"

Materials
- Drawing paper
- Crayons
- Markers
- Chart paper
- Paste

Have the students identify the food words in "Instant Indigestion." Then, have them draw an illustration to go with each food word and label the picture. On a large chart, let the class create a "Food Dictionary." Have the students paste their illustrations on the chart in alphabetical order, and have them write a description of each food beside the illustration.

Reaching Across the Curriculum

Expanding Social Studies

Activity

Objective
- to create an ethnic cookbook

Materials
- Duplicating masters
- Pens

Encourage *all* students to bring in a favorite recipe from home. Provide duplicating masters so that the recipes can be carefully copied in class, duplicated, and collated into a "Room _____'s Ethnic Cookbook." The actual collection of the duplicated recipes can lead to a discussion on the makeup of a book. **How shall we organize our cookbook? Should we have a table of contents?**

After the cookbook is "bound," lead the students in one or more of the following:

exploring measurement concepts (math)
researching recipe origins (social studies)
illustrating and describing prepared dishes (art and language)

Examining Nutritional Concepts

Activity

Objective
- to discuss nutritious foods

Materials
- Pages 47-48 in student book

Tell the students that although the poem "Instant Indigestion" is funny and imaginative, it contains foods that are not nutritious. Explain the meaning of the word "nutritious." Emphasize the importance of eating foods that keep their bodies strong and healthy. Discuss the four food groups and how much of each food group they should have every day. Then, tell them to look at the poem again. Have them find examples of foods that are not nutritious. Discuss why they're not nutritious.

Lesson 17

Sir Smasham Uppe

Disaster strikes when Sir Smasham Uppe comes to visit! This accident-prone guest should rattle funny bones as your students share the humorous results of his clumsy antics.

Objectives:

Students will
- practice choral/oral reading.
- relate personal experiences to the theme of the poem.
- increase understanding of the use of punctuation.
- extend language and ideas through oral and written expression.

Warming Up for Reading

Materials
- Chalkboard and chalk

On the chalkboard, write the word *clumsy*. Then, drop a piece of chalk on the floor. **Whoops! That was really clumsy of me!**

Walk across the room and pretend to bump into or trip over something. *That* **was really clumsy of me! How would** *you* **act out the word "clumsy"? Show us!** Choose several students to pantomime clumsy actions.

I guess everybody has experiences that make them feel clumsy. Can you think of anything that's ever happened to embarrass you because of clumsiness? Accept the students' responses. **Things like that have happened to all of us. If we were going to give a prize for "Clumsiest of the Year," it would probably go to the character in this poem, Sir Smasham Uppe. As you can probably figure out from his name,** *bad* **things happen when he's around. As I read the poem, imagine what it would be like to invite him to visit our room.**

Sharing the Poem

Materials
- Pages 50-51 in student book

Read the poem in a clipped, conversational fashion. If possible, read the poem with a bit of an English accent.

Sir Smasham Uppe

Good afternoon, Sir Smasham Uppe!
We're having tea: do take a cup.
Sugar and milk? Now let me see —
Two lumps, I think? . . . Good gracious me!
The silly thing slipped off your knee!
Pray don't apologize, old chap:
A very trivial mishap!
So clumsy of you? How absurd!
My dear Sir Smasham, not a word!
Now do sit down and have another,
And tell us all about your brother —
You know, the one who broke his head.
Is the poor fellow still in bed? —
A chair — allow me, sir! . . . Great Scott!
That *was* a nasty smash! Eh, what?
Oh, not at all: the chair was old —
Queen Anne, or so we have been told.
We've got at least a dozen more:
Just leave the pieces on the floor.
I want you to admire our view:
Come nearer to the window, do;
And look how beautiful . . . Tut, tut!
You didn't see that it was shut?
I hope you are not badly cut!

(continued)

Not hurt? A fortunate escape!
Amazing! Not a single scrape!
And now, if you have finished tea,
I fancy you might like to see
A little thing or two I've got.
That china plate? Yes, worth a lot:
A beauty too . . . Ah, there it goes!
I trust it didn't hurt your toes?
Your elbow brushed it off the shelf?
Of course, I've done the same myself.
And now, my dear Sir Smasham — Oh,
You surely don't intend to go?
You *must* be off? Well, do come again.
So glad you're fond of porcelain!

by E. V. Rieu

How does the language in the poem give you clues as to where it takes place? Point out that terms like "having tea" and "old chap" are common British expressions.

Why does Sir Smasham Uppe deserve the "Clumsiest of the Year" award? Who is the person talking in the poem? How does this person react to Sir Smasham Uppe's unusual behavior? How would you react?

What does the host mean by saying "a very trivial mishap"? Explain to the students that this means a small accident.

What do you think the host means when he says, "so glad you're fond of porcelain"? Explain that porcelain is a type of china, and the host probably said that to be sarcastic.

How do you think the host feels after Sir Smasham Uppe leaves? How do you think Sir Smasham Uppe feels?

Turn to page 50 in your book. Look at the picture. Why does Sir Smasham Uppe have that expression on his face? What's about to happen to the cup and saucer? Look at the picture on page 51. What is Sir Smasham Uppe leaving behind him? Let's read the poem together. As we read aloud, imagine that you are actually speaking to

Sir Smasham Uppe, using the voice you use when speaking to a friend. Pay attention to the punctuation in this poem. It's very important. Have the class read the poem aloud a couple of times, emphasizing punctuation and using conversational voices.

Putting Ideas to Work

Things to Talk About

Material
- Page 52 in student book

Look at page 52 in your book. "Things to Talk About" asks us to do some thinking about Sir Smasham Uppe and clumsiness.

Read number 1 with me. "Why is 'Sir Smasham Uppe' a good name for this guest?"

Possible student response — He is always smashing things up.

Read number 2 with me. "Why would you advise someone to take out insurance before inviting Sir Smasham Uppe to visit?"

Possible student response — Sir Smasham Uppe will probably accidentally destroy things in the person's house.

Read number 3 with me. "What do you think the person Sir Smasham Uppe was visiting will tell a good friend about the visit?" The host in this poem will probably be anxious to tell someone about Sir Smasham Uppe's crazy visit! What do you think the host will say about this visit?

Some possible student responses
a. "I'm never inviting that klutz over again!"
b. "I sure feel sorry for that clumsy Sir Smasham Uppe."
c. "I can't talk for long because I have to fix a broken chair, a broken window, and a broken plate."

Read number 4 with me. "Has there ever been a time when you caused an accident because you weren't careful? Tell about it." I remember once when I . . . Share a personal experience with the students, or make one up. Then, have the students tell about clumsy accidents they've had.

Things to Do

Materials
- Pages 50-52 in student book
- Writing paper
- Pencils
- Drawing paper
- Crayons

Look at the "Things to Do" on page 52 in your book. Ask each student to choose one of the three activities to do, or pick one for the whole class to do.

Let's read number 1 together. "Imagine that Sir Smasham Uppe has two children, Sam and Suzi Smasham Uppe. His children tend to have accidents just like he does. Describe what might take place if you invited the Smasham Uppe children to have dinner at your house." Have the students write stories about a dinner with Sam and Suzi Smasham Uppe.

Let's read number 2 together. "Copy your favorite four lines from the poem *without* putting in the punctuation. How does this change the way someone might read the poem? Explain why punctuation is important for making sense of what we read. See if a friend can add the necessary punctuation to your four lines." If the students seem unsure of what is meant by "punctuation," have them turn to the poem and point out some of the punctuation. Then, have each student copy four lines from the poem on paper, leaving out the punctuation. Read aloud four lines from the poem without pausing for punctuation. Lead a class discussion about the importance of punctuation before dividing the class into pairs to add punctuation to the lines they've written from the poem.

Let's read number 3 together. "Fold a piece of drawing paper in half. On one half, draw a picture that shows the room in the poem *before* Sir Smasham Uppe visits. On the other half, draw the same room *after* Sir Smasham Uppe has been there." Have the students draw *before* and *after* pictures of the room.

Extending Language and Thinking

Activity 1

Objective
- to provide alternative expressions for the poem

Materials
- Chalkboard and chalk

Why is the use of punctuation so important in this poem? Explain that the poet uses punctuation to add expression to first-person dialogue.

Why does the poet use so many exclamation points? What words and expressions in the poem have exclamation points? Point out phrases from the poem such as "Good gracious me!" and "Great Scott!" **These are not familiar terms to most of us. If *you* wanted to express dismay or concern about Sir Smasham Uppe's behavior, what are some words or expressions that you could use?** Write the students' responses on the chalkboard.

Activity 2

Objective
- to initiate new dialogue using the theme of the poem

Materials
- Chalkboard and chalk
- Writing paper
- Pencils

Let's pretend that we invited Sir Smasham Uppe to visit our class to tell us about life in England. Given his behavior in the poem, what would you expect to happen during his visit? Write the students' responses on the chalkboard.

Now, it's time to create your own versions of what occurs during a visit to our room by the one-and-only Sir Smasham Uppe. Follow the pattern of the poem by writing as if you are the host talking to Sir Smasham Uppe as he creates chaos in Room _____ . Have the students work in pairs to develop dialogue. Emphasize the need for using appropriate punctuation. Upon completion, let each pair present their new version to the rest of the class. One member of each pair should read the poem aloud, while the other pantomimes Sir Smasham Uppe's actions.

Strengthening Language for Second-Language Learners

Activity 1

Objective
- to practice using ending punctuation marks

Materials
- Index cards
- Marker
- Chalkboard and chalk

Prepare a set of three index cards for each student. Label the cards with ending punctuation marks. Put an exclamation point on one, a question mark on another, and a period on the last. On the chalkboard, write a series of brief, unpunctuated statements. As you point to each statement, ask the students to hold up the appropriate ending punctuation card. Encourage the students to explain their choices.

Activity 2

Objective
- to discuss confusing expressions and their meanings

Materials
- Chart paper
- Marker

Discuss how unfamiliar exclamatory expressions can be very confusing. Ask the students which common English exclamations puzzle them. With the students' help, create a chart of confusing expressions that the students have often heard or read. Discuss the meaning of the expressions with them.

Reaching Across the Curriculum
Developing Creative Expression

Activity 1

Objective
- to write about a clumsy experience

Materials
- Writing paper
- Pencils

Write about an experience that you have had when your clumsiness caused an accident. What happened? Could it have been avoided? How? How did people react? How did you feel? Tell the students to answer all these questions in their stories.

Activity 2

Objective
- to write creative notes

Materials
- Writing paper
- Pencils

Do you think the host in the poem will ever invite Sir Smasham Uppe back? Imagine that you are Sir Smasham Uppe. Write a note to the host apologizing for the damage you created. Make up excuses for the accidents. Then, imagine that you are the host. Write a response to Sir Smasham Uppe offering advice that suggests how he can control his clumsiness.

Expanding Social Studies

Activity

Objective
- to identify qualities of a *Good Host* and a *Good Guest*

Materials
- Writing paper
- Pencils

What was admirable about the behavior of Sir Smasham Uppe's host? What good characteristics did the host display? What other way could the host have reacted to Sir Smasham Uppe's clumsiness?

Divide a piece of paper into two columns. At the top of one column, write *A Good Guest*. At the top of the other column, write *A Good Host*. List some qualities in each column that you think are important for each individual. Once the students have completed their lists, have them share the lists with the rest of the class.

Exploring Science

Activity

Objective
- to formulate ways to avoid household accidents

Materials
- Writing paper
- Pencils

This poem pokes fun at Sir Smasham Uppe's clumsiness. We might say that he is *accident-prone*. What does this term mean? Is it possible for people like Sir Smasham Uppe to avoid accidents? Can you and your family avoid accidents? Are there accidents just waiting to happen around your house? Make a list of some of the common household accidents that occur at your house. Describe how each of the accidents might be avoided.

Lesson 18

I'm So Mad I Could Scream!

Blowing off steam is an activity that has great appeal for students and teachers! "I'm So Mad I Could Scream!" serves as a humorous catalyst for discussing feelings.

Objectives:

Students will
- describe their own emotional reactions.
- practice choral/oral reading.
- engage in problem solving.
- capture feelings in written expression.
- extend language and ideas through oral and written expression.

Warming Up for Reading

Materials
- Chalkboard and chalk
- Writing paper
- Pencils

(Using loud voice) **I'm so mad I could scream! See if you can guess what might have made me this angry.** Accept the students' responses.

Your guesses tell me that you know how it feels to be mad enough to scream! I'll tell you what made me angry *after* you share a time when something made you angry.

On the chalkboard, write *I was mad enough to scream because _____ .*

Finish this sentence on a piece of paper. Write the whole sentence, and be sure to write it in a way that will make it easy for someone else to read because we'll be trading these to share out loud. Allow time for the students to complete their sentences. Encourage them to write their messages legibly.

Now, trade papers with a partner and read silently. See if you have any questions to ask each other. Then, let's share our sentences with the whole class. Take time to let each student read her sentence aloud.

Let me tell you what made me angry. Share a personal experience with the students. **Why do other people get angry? Think about that while I share a new poem with you. It's about someone your age who is mad enough to scream, but this boy comes up with a different way of getting rid of anger.**

Sharing the Poem

Materials
- Page 53 in student book
- Chalkboard and chalk
- Writing paper
- Pencils
- Students' papers from **Warming Up for Reading**

Read the poem expressively to the students.

I'm So Mad I Could Scream!

I'm so mad I could scream,
I'm so mad I could spit,
Turn over a table,
Run off in a snit!

I'm so mad I could yell,
I could tear out my hair,
Throw a rock through a window,
Or wrestle a bear!

I mean — I am furious,
In a terrible huff,
I'm raging and roaring
And boy, am I tough!

(continued)

> I'm really ferocious,
> I really am **mad**,
> I'm ready to beat up
> My mother and dad!
>
> On thinking it over,
> **I will not** leave home,
> But I'll put all my anger
> Right here in this poem.
>
> I'm feeling much better —
> Likes peaches and cream —
> For a poem is the best way
> Of letting off steam!
>
> *by William Cole*

What did the character in the poem do about anger? What do *you* do to let off steam when you're mad? After you've had a chance to read the poem, we'll make up a list of all the ways we can get rid of anger. One way would be to let our voices express our anger! Turn to page 53 in your book. Look at the picture of the boy and the bear. Is the boy hugging the bear? Why is he wrestling with the bear? How can you tell he's angry? Can you find some words in the poem that indicate how angry he's feeling? What does the word "ferocious" mean? On the chalkboard, list the words that indicate anger.

Follow along as I read through the poem once more. Then, we'll read the whole poem together. After that, I'll pick some volunteers who think they can capture the feeling of being angry. Read the poem several times together. Then, pick individual students to read the poem expressively.

Most of our read-aloud poetry has a chorus that is repeated. This one doesn't. I don't think the poet would mind if we created our own chorus, a part that we could chant after each stanza. Think of some words that communicate anger. I'll list them on the chalkboard. Then, maybe you can figure out a way to combine some of them into a chorus that we can chant.

On the chalkboard, list words that mean you're angry. (For example, *furious, upset, outraged,* etc.) Have the students suggest combinations that could make up a rhythmic chorus. Then, read the poem again together inserting the new chorus.

The boy in our poem had a solution for anger. Would that solution work for you? Well, how *do* you blow off steam when something makes you angry? Let's break into groups and take about ten minutes to come up with a list of ways to handle anger. Divide the class into clusters of four or five students. Appoint a scribe for each group. Allow about ten minutes for group brainstorming.

Let's see what your group listed for ways to handle anger. The rest of us will react to your solutions. Are they practical or impractical? Would the solution work for us or would it get us in trouble? Would the solution help us feel better? Have the students discuss some of the suggested solutions to anger.

Now that we've talked about some of the ways that people try to get rid of their anger, look at your original paper, the one in which you finished the sentence *I was mad enough to scream because* _____ . Stretch that sentence into a paragraph. Give us some more details about why you were mad. Then, write a second paragraph that tells us either how you got rid of your anger or how you might have gotten rid of your anger. If you want this to be personal between you and me, that's okay.

Putting Ideas to Work

Things to Talk About

Material
- Page 54 in student book

Look at page 54 in your book. "Things to Talk About" asks us to do some thinking about anger.

Read the first set of questions with me. "Why do you think the person in this poem was angry? What might have caused the anger?"

Some possible student responses
a. He lost his lucky baseball cap.
b. Someone scratched his new bike.
c. His parents won't let him sleep over at his friend's house.

Read the second set of questions with me. "What do you think about the way the person in this poem lets off steam? Would that work for you? Why? Why not?"

Some possible student responses
a. Yes, writing a poem is a good way to let your feelings out.
b. No, I would have too much energy that needed to be released.

Read the third question with me. "What makes _you_ angry?" Anger is just one of the many emotions we feel. No one really likes to be angry, but sometimes things can happen that make a person mad enough to scream! Tell about one thing that makes you feel this way. Have the students talk about what makes them angry.

Things To Do

Materials
- Page 54 in student book
- Writing paper
- Pencils

Look at the "Things to Do" on page 54 in your book. Ask each student to choose one of the three activities to do, or pick one for the whole class to do.

Let's read number 1 together. "The person in this poem uses poetry to let off steam. What other emotions does a good poem make you feel? List some emotions that result from reading poetry." Help the students understand that poetry can make you feel happy, sad, excited, thoughtful, etc. Have the students write these emotions on a piece of paper.

Let's read number 2 together. "How does it feel to have someone mad at you? Write about a time when you did something to make someone angry. How did the person get over being angry with you?" Have the students write about times when they made people angry.

Let's read number 3 together. "What other emotions do people show? Make a list of different emotions that you've experienced." Have the students list emotions that they have experienced.

Extending Language and Thinking

Activity

Objectives
- to brainstorm synonyms for emotions
- to write about situations that evoke emotions

Materials
- Chalkboard and chalk
- Writing paper
- Pencils

On the chalkboard, write _anger_. This poem offers the opportunity to generate synonyms for various emotions. A natural place to start is with words that express _anger_. Ask the students to name other words that mean the same as _anger_. List these words on the chalkboard.

Then, ask the students to name other kinds of emotional reactions such as _sadness, happiness,_ and _surprise_. Write their suggestions on the chalkboard. Then, divide the class into groups of four or five students. Select a different emotion for each group. Suggest that each group come up with synonyms for the emotion they have been given. This could lead to a writing activity in which each student describes a situation evoking an emotion.

Strengthening Language for Second-Language Learners

Activity 1

Objectives
- to identify emotions through facial expressions
- to illustrate emotional situations

Materials
- Chalkboard and chalk
- Drawing paper
- Crayons

Our faces often reflect how we are feeling inside. Ask the students to try to identify various emotions by studying your facial expressions. Demonstrate happiness, displeasure, sadness, shock, and confusion. On the chalkboard, list the words that describe each emotion. Ask each student to draw a picture that illustrates a situation that would cause a person to feel one of the emotions.

Activity 2

Objective
- to promote understanding of the contractions *I'm* and *I'll*

Materials
- Chalkboard and chalk

This poem offers opportunities to develop the concept of contractions that use *I*. *I'm* and *I'll* are shortcuts for *I am* and *I will*. On the chalkboard, write *I am* and *I will*. Have the students find the contractions for these words in the poem.

On the chalkboard, write the following sentence frames, and ask the students to supply the missing contraction.

_____ *see you tomorrow.*
_____ *so sad I could cry.*
_____ *not feeling well today.*
_____ *go home after school.*

Reaching Across the Curriculum

Developing Creative Expression

Activity 1

Objective
- to create a variety of sentences expressing emotions

Materials
- Chalkboard and chalk
- Writing paper and pencils

Write the following sentence frame on the chalkboard.

I'm so _____ I could _____ .

Encourage the students to write five different versions of this sentence frame, substituting different emotions.

Activity 2

Objective
- to write about the relationship of colors to emotions

Materials
- Writing paper and pencils

Emotions are often associated with colors. Red signifies anger. Green conveys envy, and black expresses depression. Ask each student to select a color and write about how the color relates to a certain feeling.

Expanding Social Studies

Activity

Objective
- to discuss emotions

Material
- None

Lead a class discussion about feelings and emotions.

Is it okay to get angry? to cry? to be afraid? Do all people feel these emotions? How do different people handle these emotions? Are there some ways of dealing with emotions that are better than others?

Lesson 19

The Triantiwontigongolope

Ever wonder how scientists come up with those long and awkward names for plants and animals? This tongue-twisting description of a little insect may not help answer that question, but the poem should challenge the imaginations and verbal dexterity of your students.

Objectives:

Students will
- create imaginative names for new insects.
- practice choral/oral reading.
- vividly describe a triantiwontigongolope.
- extend language and ideas through oral and written expression.

Warming Up for Reading

Materials
- Chalkboard and chalk

On the chalkboard, write the words *platypus, tarantula, orangutan,* and *aardvark.*

Take a look at the unusual names on the chalkboard. See if you can describe the picture that comes to mind as I read each animal's name. Read each animal name, and then have the students say each name as you point to it. Ask the students to tell you anything they know about these animals.

Can you think of any other *odd* animal names that we can add to this list? Write the students' responses on the chalkboard. **Who do you think makes up names for animals?**

Imagine for a moment that you are a scientist and that you have discovered a very rare and previously unknown insect. Since you're the first one to discover this insect, you get to think up a name for it. Divide the class into pairs and instruct each pair to make up a name for a newly discovered insect. Then, have the students share these names and discuss why they chose them.

Today, we're going to put your scientific curiosity to work. You're going to meet a unique creature who has been given an incredible name. This creature is so rare that very few scientists have actually seen it. You'll be among the first to hear and read about it. Listen carefully as I read, and see if you can picture this creature in your mind.

Sharing the Poem

Materials
- Page 55 in student book
- Chalkboard and chalk

Read the poem aloud to the students. Be sure to carefully pronounce "tri-anti-wonti-gon-go-lope."

(Turn the page for the poem.)

The Triantiwontigongolope

First Child:	There's a very funny insect that you do not often spy,
Second Child:	And it isn't quite a spider, and it isn't quite a fly;
First Child:	It is something like a beetle, and a little like a bee,
Second Child:	But nothing like a woolly grub that climbs upon a tree.
First Child:	Its name is quite a hard one, but you'll learn it soon, I hope.
First Child:	So, try:
Chorus:	Tri—
All:	Tri—anti—wonti—
Children:	Triantiwontigongolope

by C. J. Dennis

I warned you that this creature had an incredible name! I'll write it on the chalkboard, so you can read it with me. On the chalkboard, write *tri-anti-wonti-gon-go-lope*. With the students, slowly read the word aloud several times.

What *is* a triantiwontigongolope? Do you think it is a real insect? Why or why not?

If you were to draw a picture of a triantiwontigongolope for a scientific journal, what would your drawing look like? Listen as I read through the poem again to pick up clues about what this insect looks like. This time, I'll stop after pronouncing parts of the insect's name so that you can say it back to me. Read the poem aloud allowing sufficient time for the students to repeat the parts of the insect's name.

Now, which clues from the poem would help you draw an accurate picture of this insect? Turn to page 55 in your book. Look at the picture of the triantiwontigongolope. Does it look anything like what you had imagined?

This poem is a *real* tongue twister! Let's read it together a few times. See if you can find more details about the insect. Have the class practice reading the poem in unison. Then, pick one student to be the first child and one student to be the second child. Assign reading the chorus to the rest of the class. Have the students read the poem again chiming in on their assigned parts.

Putting Ideas to Work

Things to Talk About

Material
- Page 56 in student book

Look at page 56 in your book. "Things to Talk About" asks us to do some thinking about the triantiwontigongolope.

Read number 1 with me. "What would be your first reaction if you were to find a triantiwontigongolope? Would you be afraid to pick it up?"

Some possible student responses
a. I'd pick it up and add it to my bug collection.
b. I'd scream and run away because I don't like bugs.
c. I'd get my camera and take a picture of it. I wouldn't be afraid to pick it up.

Read number 2 with me. "There are *helpful* insects and *harmful* insects. In what ways might the triantiwontigongolope be *helpful*? How might it be *harmful*?"
Discuss how the triantiwontigongolope might be *helpful* or *harmful*.

Some possible student responses
a. Helpful — It might eat harmful insects.
b. Harmful — It might give a bad sting.

Read number 3 with me. "How would you describe this insect to a person who has never seen it?" The poem doesn't give us a lot of details about the triantiwontigongolope but use the picture to help you.

Some possible student responses
a. It's big and has eight green legs.
b. It has two wings and large round eyes.
c. It has white dots on its body.

Things to Do

Materials
- Pages 55-56 in student book
- Drawing paper
- Crayons
- Writing paper
- Pencils

Look at the "Things to Do" on page 56 in your book. Ask each student to choose one of the three activities to do, or pick one for the whole class to do.

Let's read number 1 together. "Get four or five members of your class to work with you. Divide the poem into parts and practice reading it aloud. Then, present the poem to younger students, and ask them to draw pictures of a triantiwontigongolope."
Have the students present the poem to others. When the students complete their presentation, tell them to give out drawing paper and crayons to their audience so that the audience can draw pictures of the triantiwontigongolope.

Let's read number 2 together. "Make believe that you are a scientist who discovers a new animal. Make up a long name for this animal. Write a newspaper article that tells what it looks like, how you found it, and where you found it. Draw a picture of the animal to go with your newspaper article."
Have the students write about their newly discovered animals and draw pictures of them.

Let's read number 3 together. "Look up the definition of *insect*. Write a brief definition of *insect* in your own words. Then, write down the names of all the insects you know. See how many insect names you can recall." Have each student write the definition of *insect* and list all the names of insects that they can recall.

Extending Language and Thinking

Activity

Objectives
- to recall details from the poem
- to write about a triantiwontigongolope
- to draw pictures of a triantiwontigongolope

Materials
- Chalkboard and chalk
- Drawing paper
- Crayons
- Writing paper
- Pencils

On the chalkboard, write *insect.*

We've discovered that the triantiwontigongolope is a kind of insect. What do we know about insects? List the students' responses on the chalkboard.

Draw two columns on the chalkboard. At the top of one column, write *Like* and at the top of the other, write *Unlike.*

What does the poem tell us that the triantiwontigongolope is "something like" or "a little like"? On the chalkboard, list the students' responses under *Like.*

What does the poem tell us that the triantiwontigongolope "isn't quite" like or "nothing like"? On the chalkboard, list the students' responses under *Unlike.*

Entomologists are scientists who study insects. They often draw sketches of the insects they are studying. Let's pretend that we are entomologists who have just discovered the very rare triantiwontigongolope. Using the information on the chalkboard, sketch a picture of what you think this insect looks like. After you've sketched a triantiwontigongolope, write a short paragraph about this insect. Describe *what* it looks like, *where* it's found, and *how* it is helpful and harmful.

Once the students have completed their sketches and paragraphs, divide the class into groups. The students should share their paragraphs with the other members of their groups. Group members are responsible for telling one good thing about each description and suggesting one idea that might help improve the description. Once the students have received this constructive criticism, have them revise their paragraphs and come up with final copies.

Strengthening Language for Second-Language Learners

Activity

Objectives
- to divide nonsense words into syllables
- to identify vowel sounds

Materials
- Chalkboard and chalk

On the chalkboard, write *triantiwontigongolope*. Point to the word. **Pronounce this word with me. TRI-AN-TI-WON-TI-GON-GO-LOPE. Let's break this word into its parts or syllables. Every syllable must have a vowel sound you hear. Who can come up and draw lines between the syllables as we pronounce the word?** Have a volunteer separate the word into syllables as the rest of the class *slowly* reads the word aloud.

How many syllables did we come up with? What is the vowel sound you hear in the first syllable? in the second? Point to each syllable in the word, and have the students pronounce and identify the vowel sound.

On the chalkboard, write the following nonsense words.

tradongolongmobote (tra-don-go-long-mo-bote)
driantokosodobe (dri-an-to-ko-so-dobe)
blidehinaficlate (bli-de-hi-na-fi-clate)

Pronounce each word, and divide it into syllables. Then, have the students identify the vowel sound in each syllable.

Have each student make up his own nonsense word using these words as models. Let each student write his word on the chalkboard and challenge the other students to pronounce it.

Reaching Across the Curriculum

Exploring Science

Activity 1

Objective
- to discuss and research the topic of insects

Materials
- Library sources
- Writing paper and pencils

The following are some interesting facts to stimulate discussion and research about insects. Have the students use library sources to find out several new facts about insects.

> According to scientists, there are about 700,000 different species of insects, and thousands of new ones are being described each year.

> Fossil records show that many species of insects exist today in much the same form as they did 200 million years ago.

> The survival success of insects is attributed to their small size, their high reproductive rate, and the wonderfully adaptive abilities of the group as a whole.

> *The New Columbia Encyclopedia*
> (New York: Columbia University Press, 1975), pp. 1343-1344.

Activity 2

Objective
- to research specific topics about insects

Materials
- Library sources
- Writing paper
- Pencils
- Bulletin board

Divide the class into research groups. Assign each group a set of questions to research from the following list. Brief research reports can be written, shared, and posted on the bulletin board.

1. What insects are harmful to our food supply? Do any harmful insects live in our community? What are they?

2. What insects are helpful? How are they helpful? What helpful insects live in our community?

3. What insects are dangerous to people? How are they dangerous? What dangerous insects live in our community? What precautions should we take when we see these insects?

4. How can harmful insects be controlled? What are some dangers of using insecticides to control harmful insects?

Using Math

Activity

Objective
- to identify prefixes denoting numerical values

Materials
- Chalkboard and chalk
- Dictionaries

The word *triantiwontigongolope* contains the number prefix *tri,* meaning three. Brainstorm a list of common number prefixes with the students. On the chalkboard, write the prefixes and the quantities that they represent. Then, have the students brainstorm lists of words for each prefix. Provide them with dictionaries if necessary. The students' lists might be similar to the following.

uni — one	*bi — two*	*tri — three*
unicycle	*bifocals*	*triangle*
unilateral	*bimonthly*	*triplets*

Here's your script. Just read the bold face type.

Lesson 20

Godfrey Gordon Gustavus Gore

Annoying habits can get us into trouble! Godfrey Gordon is threatened with dire punishment in this funny rhyme that hits close to home for all of us.

Objectives:

Students will
- share personal experiences related to the poem.
- interpret the actions of characters in the poem.
- participate in choral/oral reading.
- analyze the consequences of behavior.
- extend language and ideas through oral and written expression.

Warming Up for Reading

Materials
- Chalkboard and chalk

On the chalkboard, write the following sentences.

Go to bed!
Get off the phone!
Clean your room!

Is there anything familiar about what I've written on the chalkboard? Give me a "thumbs up" if anybody has ever said those things to you! I guess times don't change. Those are the same words my parents used to say to me over and over again. I got sick of hearing them! How about you? Are there other expressions that your family says over and over to you that really bug you? What are they? List the students' responses on the chalkboard.

There is one expression that nobody's mentioned. I'd better add it to our list. On the chalkboard, write *Shut the door!* **I'm sure you've heard me say that occasionally! There's a character in our poem today who has some real problems with hearing that command over and over again. That's not**

the only problem he has. His name is quite a mouthful! It's Godfrey Gordon Gustavus Gore. See if you can identify with Godfrey's problem.

Sharing the Poem

Materials
- Chalkboard and chalk
- Pages 57-58 in student book

Read the poem to the students with exaggerated expression.

Godfrey Gordon Gustavus Gore

Godfrey Gordon Gustavus Gore —
No doubt you have heard the name before —
Was a boy who never would shut a door!

The wind might whistle, the wind might roar,
And teeth be aching and throats be sore,
But still he never would shut the door.

His father would beg, his mother implore,
"Godfrey Gordon Gustavus Gore,
We really **do** wish you would shut the door!"

Their hands they wrung, their hair they tore;
But Godfrey Gordon Gustavus Gore
Was deaf as the boards upon the floor.

When he walked forth the folks would roar,
"Godfrey Gordon Gustavus Gore,
Why don't you think to shut the door?"

They rigged out a small raft with sail and oar,
And threatened to pack off Gustavus Gore
On a deep sea voyage to Singapore.

(continued)

But he begged for mercy, and said, "No more!
Pray do not send me to Singapore
On a small raft, and then I will shut the door!"

"You will?" said his parents; "then keep on shore!
But mind you do! For the seat is sore
Of a fellow that never will shut the door,
Godfrey Gordon Gustavus Gore!"

*Adaptation of a poem
by William Brighty Rands*

What command got Godfrey in trouble? On the chalkboard, underline *Shut the door!* **What's Godfrey's last name?** Add a comma and *Gore* to the phrase *Shut the door.* Now, it will read *Shut the door, Gore.*

What kind of punctuation mark should I add to indicate a strong demand? Add an exclamation mark to *Shut the door, Gore.* **As I read the poem again,** I'll pause after each stanza so that you can chime in with the chorus, *Shut the door, Gore!* **Let's try it once for practice.** Read the poem again, with the students providing the chorus.

What threat did Godfrey's parents make to get him to shut the door? Do you think they would have really carried through with their threat?

Turn to page 57 in your book. **Look at the picture. What is Godfrey doing? What has he forgotten to do?** Turn to page 58. **Look at the picture** on page 58. **What do the words on the sail say? Where do you think the raft is going?**

Look at the words that end each line of the poem. What do you notice about the words? Yes, they all rhyme even if they're not spelled the same way. What are some different ways of spelling the /or/ sound? Encourage the students to name the different rhyming words in the poem. Write these words on the chalkboard.

This poem will make a good "Readers' Theater." Let's practice it together, and then we'll let volunteers be the narrator, Godfrey, and the parents. The volunteers will come to the front of the room to present this sad tale. Read the poem aloud with the students several times before having individuals take the parts of the narrator, Father, Mother, and Godfrey. For the "Readers' Theater," each participant should turn her back to the audience and face the audience only when she is speaking her part.

Putting Ideas to Work

Things to Talk About

Material

- Page 59 in student book

Look at page 59 in your book. "Things to Talk About" asks us to do some thinking about Godfrey and his problem.

Read the first question with me. "How old do you think Godfrey is?"

Some possible student responses — 5, 8, 13

Read the second question with me. "Do you think Godfrey left the door open on purpose? Why? Why not?"

Some possible student responses
a. Yes, he likes being a pest.
b. No, he's just very forgetful.

Read the third question with me. "Do you think Godfrey will remember to shut the door next time?" **Godfrey doesn't seem able to remember to shut the door behind him. I wonder if the threat of a long and lonely trip to Singapore will help him remember next time. What do you think?**

Possible student responses — yes, no

Read the fourth question with me. "Does this poem remind you of something that has happened to you?"

Some possible student responses
a. Yes, I always forget to shut the door.
b. No, I don't have to be reminded to shut the door.

Things to Do

Materials
- Page 59 in student book
- Writing paper
- Pencils
- Drawing paper
- Markers
- Chalkboard and chalk

Look at the "Things to Do" on page 59 in your book. Ask each student to choose one of the three activities to do, or pick one for the whole class to do. *Do all 3.*

Let's read number 1 together. "Forgetting to shut the door may not be Godfrey's only problem. What other annoying habits might this mischievous young boy have? Write about how these annoying habits get Godfrey into trouble." Have the students write about Godfrey's annoying habits and how they get him into trouble.

a paragraph or two

Let's read number 2 together. "Make a reminder sign to put on Godfrey's door that will remind him of his responsibility." Have the students make signs that will remind Godfrey to shut the door.

Let's read number 3 together. "Sometimes there are good reasons for leaving doors open. List three good reasons." Have the students list reasons why it is sometimes good to leave doors open. Then, have them share their ideas with the rest of the class. On the chalkboard, list some of the most important reasons offered by the students.

End of lesson. Kids who finish early can share their work in front of class while others are still working. Collect. Save on front table. Name on them!!!

Extending Language and Thinking

Activity 1

Objective
- to develop alternative solutions for a problem

Materials
- Writing paper
- Pencils

Do you think it was fair for his family to scold Godfrey? What was so important about shutting the door in the first place? Write down three good reasons why it is important to make sure doors are shut.

Okay, let's see what the Gores had in mind by scolding Godfrey. Why was it necessary to shut the door? Have the students share reasons from the lists they have generated. **Was it necessary to *threaten* Godfrey? Could there have been some other solution? What would you have done if Godfrey was your child?** Encourage the students to offer alternative solutions for the problem.

Activity 2

Objective
- to share personal experiences about behaviors in need of change

Materials
- Chalkboard and chalk
- Writing paper
- Pencils

Sometimes threats work and sometimes they don't. I remember once when I . . . Share a childhood experience involving a threat made to try to change your behavior. **How about you? Did you ever have someone in your family threaten you so that you would change an annoying behavior? Think about it and then complete these sentences.** Write the following sentence frames on the chalkboard.

Once I was supposed to _____ . When I didn't do it, my _____ threatened to _____ .

That's just the beginning! We want to know what happened. Did you do what you were supposed to do? Did you get punished? Did the threat change your behavior? Would there have been a better way to get you to change? I bet we'll all relate to each other's experiences when we talk about them. Encourage the students to develop paragraphs about their personal experiences. Then, divide the class into groups of four or five students. Have each student share her paragraph with the others in her group. Suggest that each group select the most unique experiences to share with the entire class. This writing activity could lead to a discussion of the advantages and disadvantages of making threats and a discussion of alternative solutions for changing behavior.

Activity 3

Objectives
- to discuss names
- to make up names

Materials
- Writing paper
- Pencils

Why in the world would Mr. and Mrs. Gore name their child "Godfrey Gordon Gustavus"? Where *do* people come up with names for children? What are some of the most unusual names you've ever heard? What are some of your favorite names? How do you feel about your own name?

Use the last names of some students in our class. Think up at least three first names to go with each of the last names of the students. The three first names should all begin with the same letter as the last name. Remember that the renaming is all in fun!

Strengthening Language for Second-Language Learners

Activity 1

Objective
- to identify different spellings for the same sound

Materials
- Chart paper
- Marker

Words that sound alike are not necessarily spelle[...] The poem "Godfrey Gordon Gust[...] [illust]rates this principle. Enc[...] find various spellings for [...] [s]pellings on a ch[...] [sou]nds in the [...] [crea]ted by [...] to create a [...] [v]aried spellings

Ac[...]

Objective
- to discuss the us[e of punct]uation in the poem

Materials
- Pages 57-58 in student book

This poem makes use of a variety of punctuation marks. Why do these marks appear? What are their purposes? How do they help our choral reading? Using the poem in the student book, lead a class discussion about this topic. Point out various punctuation marks and why they have been used.

Reaching Across the Curriculum

Developing Creative Expression

Activity

Objective
- to create new versions of the poem

Materials
- Chalkboard and chalk
- Writing paper
- Pencils

The pattern of this poem provides a model for creating verses about other characters whose behavior is annoying. On the chalkboard, write the following model.

Betsy Bedelia Bartholomew Bloom
Was a girl who never would clean her room.
Clean your room, Bloom!

On the chalkboard, write the following sentence frames. Ask the students to develop their own verses.

_____   _____   _____   _____

Was a boy who never would go to bed.
Go to bed, _____ !

_____   _____   _____   _____

Was a girl who never would empty the trash.
Empty the trash, _____ !

Expanding Social Studies

Activity 1

Objective
- to discuss consequences of behavior

Material
- None

Do you think Godfrey was aware of what the consequences of his behavior would be? Are you always aware of what will happen when you behave a certain way? What would happen if you did any of the following?

1. **You got an "F" in reading on your report card.**
2. **You didn't finish your homework assignment.**
3. **You broke a window with a baseball.**
4. **You didn't clean your room when asked.**

Activity 2

Objective
- to identify "good" and "bad" behaviors

Materials
- Writing paper
- Pencils

Have the students divide their papers into two columns. At the top of one column, have them write *Good News*. Underneath this heading, tell them to list some behaviors that bring them praise. At the top of the second column, have the students write *Bad News* and then list behaviors that get them into trouble.

Expanding Literature

Activity

Objective
- to share children's books

Materials
- Children's books
  Silverstein, Shel. *Where the Sidewalk Ends.* New York: Harper and Row, Publishers, Inc., 1974.
  Livingston, Myra Cohn, ed. *Speak Roughly to Your Little Boy.* New York: Harcourt Brace Jovanovich, Inc., 1971.

Godfrey isn't the only young person who gets into trouble. Share "Sarah Cynthia Sylvia Stout" by Shel Silverstein from *Where the Sidewalk Ends.*

Also worth sharing are the annoying behaviors of children found in *Speak Roughly to Your Little Boy.*

Lesson 21

Fingers Anytime

Why be formal? Finger food is so much fun to eat, and it's fun to share in this rollicking rhyme that will tempt appetites and encourage involvement.

Objectives:

Students will

- relate personal food favorites.
- practice choral/oral reading.
- express personal food preferences through creative writing.
- discuss more nutritious food snacks.
- extend language and ideas through oral and written expression.

Warming Up for Reading

Materials

- Chalkboard and chalk

On the chalkboard, write the column headings *Finger Foods* and *Fork Foods*.

How hungry are you? Let's build up a big appetite for lunch/dinner by thinking of some of our favorite foods. I need five foods to put in each column. Take some time to come up with favorite foods we eat with our fingers and favorite foods we eat with a fork. Write the students' contributions under the appropriate headings.

That was easy. Which column has more of your favorites? Do you know that it is considered impolite to eat certain foods with your fingers? Obviously, the people in today's poem would prefer to eat this way. Listen to see if you agree.

Sharing the Poem

Materials

- Chalkboard and chalk
- Pages 60-61 in student book

Read the poem aloud with enthusiasm, encouraging students to chime in by rubbing their fingers together as they chant the chorus.

Fingers Anytime

Knives and forks and spoons are fine,
But I'll take fingers anytime!

**Icky, picky, sticky fingers
I'll take fingers anytime!**

Fingers for pizza that makes such a mess.
Fingers for tacos that drip on my dress.

Fingers for crispy and crunchy fried chicken,
Fingers for stuffin', fingers for lickin'.

**Icky, picky, sticky fingers
I'll take fingers anytime!**

Fingers for hot dogs that let out a squirt.
Fingers for hamburgers all over my shirt.

Fingers for french fries and popcorn and chips,
Fingers for raisins and licorice whips.

**Icky, picky, sticky fingers
I'll take fingers anytime!**

Fingers for ice cream that falls off a cone.
Fingers for spareribs that stick to a bone.

Fingers for sandwiches, bigger the better,
Fingers for cookies all over my sweater.

Yes, knives and forks and spoons are fine,
But I'll take fingers anytime!

**Icky, picky, sticky fingers
I'll take fingers anytime!**

by Barbara Schmidt

How does the poet feel about finger food? Listen again as I read through the poem once more. We'll make a list of the finger foods in the poem and vote on your favorites. Help me out with the chorus and pretend to rub your "sticky" fingers on your clothes. Read the poem again encouraging student participation.

Now, tell me the foods that were mentioned in the poem. Then, we'll vote to find your favorites. You only get one vote! I know it's a hard choice. List the foods on the chalkboard. Then, tally the students' votes to determine the class favorite.

Turn to page 60 in your book. Look at the picture. What is the person holding? Would this food make your fingers sticky? What about the food on page 61? Eating finger food isn't always a picnic! Find the parts of the poem that describe problems with finger food.

Now, let's have some finger-lickin' fun with this poem. Select groups or individuals to read each stanza aloud with mouth-watering expression.

Putting Ideas to Work

Things to Talk About

Materials
- Page 62 in student book
- Chalkboard and chalk

Look at page 62 in your book. "Things to Talk About" asks us to do some thinking about finger foods.

Read the first question with me. "What makes eating finger foods so much fun?"

Some possible student responses
a. Finger foods taste better than most foods you have to eat with silverware.
b. When you eat finger foods, you can make a mess and nobody gets mad at you.
c. With finger foods, you can lick every last bit of food off your fingers.

Read the second question with me. "What are some problems with finger foods?" Finger foods may be fun and delicious, but they can also cause problems. Can you think of some of these problems?

Some possible student responses
a. Your hands can get very sticky and gooey.
b. You might take a bite that is too big and get it all over your face.
c. You might drop food on your clothes.

Read the third question with me. "What are some other finger foods that weren't mentioned in the poem?" List the students' responses on the chalkboard.

Some possible student responses — peanuts, grapes, celery sticks

Things to Do

Materials
- Page 62 in student book
- Writing paper
- Pencils
- Chalkboard and chalk
- Drawing paper
- Crayons

Look at the "Things to Do" on page 62 in your book. Ask each student to choose one of the three activities to do, or pick one for the whole class to do.

Let's read number 1 together. "Pick your favorite food from the poem. Describe it in mouth-watering detail. Tell why it is easier to eat with your fingers than with a knife, fork, or spoon." Have the students write descriptions of their favorite foods from the poem.

Let's read number 2 together. **"Make a list of finger foods that are more healthy for you to eat than some of the ones mentioned in this poem."** The finger foods mentioned in this poem may be delicious, but many of them aren't very good for you. Think of some finger foods that are more nutritious than licorice whips and ice cream. On the chalkboard, write a list of nutritious foods the students suggest. Discuss what makes a food nutritious. Use this list as the basis for further class discussion about the importance of good nutrition.

Let's read number 3 together. **"Draw a picture of a stanza of the poem that reminds you of something that has happened to you."** Have you ever dropped ice cream from a cone or gotten cookie crumbs all over your sweater? Look at the poem for more finger food adventures like these. Draw a picture of one of these adventures. Pick one that reminds you of something that has happened to you. Have the students illustrate stanzas from the poem.

Extending Language and Thinking

Activity 1

Objective
- to share personal experiences

Material
- None

Our poem describes some of the hazards of eating finger food. Was there ever a time when you had a disastrous experience using your fingers to eat? I remember one time when . . . Share a personal experience, or make one up. Divide into teams of two and tell your partner the worst thing that ever happened to you when you were eating finger food. Have the students share personal experiences.

Activity 2

Objective
- to describe advantages of using utensils

Materials
- Writing paper
- Pencils

There are some advantages in using knives, forks, and spoons. List three important advantages of using eating utensils. Then, describe at least three foods that would be very difficult to eat with your fingers, like jello and soup.

Strengthening Language for Second-Language Learners

Activity 1

Objective
- to strengthen sight-word recognition

Materials
- Index cards
- Marker
- Drawing paper
- Crayons

This poem is filled with familiar foods. Write each food word on an index card. Encourage the students to draw pictures of these foods and to match the pictures to the appropriate word cards. Then, write *knife, fork,* and *spoon* on separate index cards. Have the students draw pictures for these words and match the pictures to the appropriate word cards.

Activity 2

Objective
- to provide practice in word meaning

Materials
- Index cards
- Marker

With the students, generate a list of words containing the "ick" sound. Write each word on an index card. Place the cards face up on a table. Tell the students that you will read some sentences to them. Explain that each sentence has a word missing. Tell them to listen carefully to each sentence, and ask them to choose one of the words on the cards to fill in the sentence. Have a student hold up the appropriate card. Say sentences similar to the following.

1. **I did not come to school today because I was _____ .** (sick)
2. **That puppy will _____ your face.** (lick)

Reaching Across the Curriculum

Developing Creative Expression

Activity

Objective
• to classify finger foods

Materials
• Chalkboard and chalk

How many categories of finger foods can your students create? Brainstorm with the students and list their suggestions on the chalkboard. Then, ask them to think of ways that these foods could be grouped. For example, the foods could be grouped as main dishes, desserts, and snacks, or as hot foods and cold foods. See what other categories the students can identify.

Expanding Social Studies

Activity

Objective
• to research eating utensils

Materials
• Library sources
• Writing paper
• Pencils

Encourage your students to research the development of eating utensils. Have them trace the history of knives, forks, and spoons. Ask them to imagine how different and messy eating might be without these implements.

Exploring Science

Activity 1

Objective
• to compare and discuss the nutritional value of snack foods

Material
• None

Fruits and vegetables are the original finger foods and are very important for good nutrition. Encourage the students to compare the nutritional value of the snack foods in the poem with the nutritional value of vegetable sticks and fresh fruits. Explain the meaning of the word "nutritious." Emphasize the importance of eating foods that keep their bodies strong and healthy. Have the students compare the calories and cost of the snack foods in the poem with the calories and cost of more nutritious snacks.

Activity 2

Objective
• to discuss cleanliness in handling food

Material
• None

Eating food with your fingers may be fun, but is it always sanitary? What are some problems that could occur with "icky, picky, sticky" unwashed fingers that touch food? A discussion on cleanliness while handling food and the danger of germs on unwashed hands may evolve from this poem.

Lesson 22

WHATILLIDO?

This familiar refrain will strike a responsive chord. At times, we've all muttered, "WHATILLIDO?" There's lots to talk about in resolving the annoying dilemma of the girl who whines in this poem!

Objectives:

Students will
- practice choral/oral reading.
- relate personal experiences to content.
- generate alternative problem-solving solutions.
- analyze how they spend their time.
- extend language and ideas through oral and written expression.

Warming Up for Reading

Materials
- Chalkboard and chalk

On the chalkboard, write *WHATILLIDO?* Be sure to link the words together as in the poem.

I know it's hard for you to ever imagine a time when you'd say the run-together words on the chalkboard. But just in case, let's practice it. Say it with me. Have the students chant the word in unison.

Let's imagine some of the following situations.

The TV is broken, and my friends are away. It's raining. I'm bored. What do I say? Point to the chalkboard. Have the students say, "WHATILLIDO?"

How about this? My papers are finished; it's not time to play. There's twenty minutes until recess. What do I say? Point to the chalkboard again. The students should chant, "WHATILLIDO?"

You got some good expression in that time! It almost sounded as if you're familiar with that word! Let's give it one more try. I'm on a long trip. I've been driving all day. I'm tired and hungry. What do I say? Point to the chalkboard again. The students should chant, "WHATILLIDO?"

You gave me such a rousing chorus! You're really ready to hear about someone who truly abuses that word! Think about whether you've ever known anyone like this character. Be sure to give me a big "WHATILLIDO?" when I come to that part of today's poem.

Sharing the Poem

Materials
- Pages 63-64 in student book

Read the poem aloud pausing for the students to chime in on the chorus.

(Turn the page for the poem.)

WHATILLIDO?

This is a true story. It's not about YOU.
There's this girl that I know who says,
"WHATILLIDO?"

She's got games, sports equipment, the latest that's new,
Yet she sits doing nothing, whines,
"WHATILLIDO?"

Her schoolwork's not finished. Her teacher turns blue
As she mumbles repeatedly,
"WHATILLIDO?"

Her aunt, feeling sorry, took her to the zoo.
She stood in the middle, sulked,
"WHATILLIDO?"

Her class took a field trip to look at the view.
She stood there, not looking, asked,
"WHATILLIDO?"

To visit her gram on an airplane she flew.
Drove everyone crazy with
"WHATILLIDO?"

Some kids on the bus spread her seat with clear glue.
When she couldn't get up, they yelled,
"WHATILLSHEDO?"

And her parents by this time were just about through,
Took a look at her stuck and shrugged,
"WHATILLWEDO?"

There's a lesson here somewhere. How's this for a clue?
Think **twice** before muttering,
"WHATILLIDO?"

by Barbara Schmidt

What do you think about the ending? Did she deserve to be left stuck to her seat? Why? Why not?

Turn to page 63 in your book. Look at the picture. What do you think the girl is saying? Turn to page 64. Why is the girl still sitting on the bus? Let's have some fun chiming along with the girl. We'll read the poem through once together, and then volunteers can select one stanza of the poem to read while we read the chorus. Before we begin, how will the chorus for the children and the parents be different from the girl's "WHATILLIDO?" Emphasize that the girl whines and sulks, while the children's and the parents' responses sound more like they're saying, "Too bad!" Read the poem together several times.

Putting Ideas to Work

Things to Talk About

Material

• Page 65 in student book

Look at page 65 in your book. "Things to Talk About" tells us to do some thinking about the behavior of the girl in the poem.

Read the first question with me. "What was this girl's problem?" Possible student response — She's always complaining and saying, "WHATILLIDO?"

Read the second question with me. "What made her constantly ask the same question?" Why do you think this girl is always asking, "WHATILLIDO?"

Some possible student responses
a. She doesn't know how to keep busy.
b. She never learned how to say anything except "WHATILLIDO?"
c. She thinks she's funny.

Read the third question with me. "Do you think she learned her lesson?" The children on the bus were trying to teach the girl a lesson when they glued her to her seat. Do you think they were successful?

Some possible student responses
a. Yes, she probably felt so stupid that she'll never again say, "WHATILLIDO?"
b. No, she'll never stop complaining no matter what.

Read the fourth set of questions with me. "Do you know anyone whose behavior reminds you of the girl in the poem? Who? How are they alike?" Have the students tell who the girl reminds them of and why.

Things to Do

Materials
• Page 65 in student book
• Writing paper
• Pencils

Look at the "Things to Do" on page 65 in your book. Ask each student to choose one of the three activities to do, or pick one for the whole class to do.

Let's read number 1 together. "Select one stanza of the poem. Make a list of at least three suggestions of things the girl could do in the situation." The girl in this poem goes to a lot of interesting places, and yet all she can think to do is stand around saying, "WHATILLIDO?" Choose one of the places she goes and write down at least three things that she could do at that place. Have the students write lists of things that the girl could do.

Let's read number 2 together. "How would you handle this girl's behavior if you were her parents? Write a letter to her parents offering your advice." Have the students write letters of advice to the girl's parents.

Let's read number 3 together. "What do *you* do when you're bored and have nothing to do? Describe a time when this happened to you and how you solved your problem." Have the students write about times when they were bored and what they did to entertain themselves.

Extending Language
and Thinking

Activity

Objective
- to extend knowledge of punctuation

Materials
- Writing paper
- Pencils
- Duplicating masters

"WHATILLIDO?" offers opportunities to talk about punctuation. Lead a class discussion about how the author of this poem uses punctuation to get the message across. Ask your students to imagine the poem without any punctuation. Have them discuss the problems that might create.

Have each student copy a stanza of the poem *without* punctuation, and tell her to pass it to a neighbor to try reading. This will also reinforce the idea that handwriting must be legible if we want to share written information with others.

Consider duplicating the situations you read in **Warming Up for Reading**. Do not put in the punctuation. Have the students work in teams of two to determine where to place the punctuation and why it should be placed there.

Strengthening Language
for Second-Language Learners

Activity 1

Objective
- to provide practice with contractions

Materials
- Index cards
- Marker
- Pages 63-64 in student book

This poem provides a good opportunity to discuss contractions. Write each of the contractions *it's, there's, she's, couldn't,* and *how's* on a separate index card. Make another set of index cards. On each card, write the two words that make up each contraction.

Hold up one of the contraction cards. Say the word on the card. Explain to the students that this is a contraction, which is a short way of combining two words. Point to the apostrophe. Explain that the apostrophe indicates that a letter or letters are missing. Ask the students to tell you the two words that make up the contraction.

Hold up the word card showing the appropriate two words.

Spread the rest of the cards on a table face up. Have the students match each contraction card with the card that shows the two words the contraction indicates. Next, have the students find each contraction in the poem and say the two words that make up the contraction. Then, hold up a contraction card and call on a student to use that contraction in a sentence.

Activity 2

Objective
- to determine the setting for the stanzas

Material
- None

The setting for many stanzas in this poem changes. Discuss with the students how to identify the location by using clues from the poem to help us determine where the action is taking place.

Reaching Across the Curriculum

Developing Creative Expression

Activity 1

Objective
- to identify other repetitious questions

Materials
- Writing paper
- Pencils
- Chalkboard and chalk

Are there other common repetitious questions that people often say? Think of some and write them down. Combine the words of the question into one long word like "WHATILLIDO?" To help the students get started, you might write the following on the chalkboard.

WHEREYAGOIN'?   WHATCHADOIN'?

Contribute your combination words to a class list. We'll call our list "I'm sick of hearing _____ ." I'll write the list on the chalkboard.

Activity 2

Objective
- to identify annoying sayings

Materials
- Writing paper
- Pencils

Think about a time when you've been guilty of saying "WHATILLIDO?" When was it? Did it get on somebody's nerves? Whose? What do people do or say that gets on your nerves? Write down a particular saying that really annoys you. Tell why it bugs you.

Expanding Social Studies

Activity

Objective
- to categorize free-time activities

Materials
- Writing paper
- Pencils

Ask the students to keep a log of how their free time is spent during a week's period. Encourage the students to analyze their activities on the basis of criteria you establish together. Have the students categorize their activities by dividing them into productive, restful, healthy, pleasurable, helpful, etc.

Fostering Good Study Habits

Activity

Objective
- to discuss time management

Material
- None

This poem offers an introduction to the important topic of time management. How do your students balance their school and study time with recreational time? What study habits are they developing that help them make the best use of their time? Are they aware of how to schedule their time wisely? Given choices, are they able to identify priorities? Encourage the students to develop schedules and discuss the results.

Lesson 23

Silly Slim Slupper

"Silly Slim Slupper" can be sung to the tune of the familiar folk song "Old Dan Tucker." The comical antics of "Silly Slim" will amuse your students.

Objectives:

Students will
- listen to the poem and visualize the character.
- compare and contrast their behavior with the behavior of the character in the poem.
- practice choral/oral reading.
- recall details and make inferences.
- create vivid descriptions of the character.
- extend language and ideas through oral and written expression.

Warming Up for Reading

Material
- None

Was there ever a time when you were late for supper? Were you ever so late that you didn't get supper? How did missing supper make you feel? What did you do?

In today's poem, you'll hear about an unusual character named Silly Slim Slupper. He not only misses supper, but also does some very strange things. As I read the poem, think of what Silly Slim Slupper looks like. Picture in your mind some of the strange things he does. What's so silly about the way Slim Slupper does things?

Sharing the Poem

Materials
- Pages 66-68 in student book
- Chalkboard and chalk

In a lively manner, read the poem aloud or sing to the tune of "Old Dan Tucker."

Silly Slim Slupper

Chorus

Stay out of the way
of Silly Slim Slupper
Mad because he missed
his supper.
Supper's over,
the dishes are clean,
And there's nothing left
but one old bean.

Silly Slim Slupper
was a funny man.
He washed his face
in a frying pan.
He combed his hair
with a wagon wheel
And brushed his teeth
with a piece of steel.

Chorus

Stay out of the way
of Silly Slim Slupper
Mad because he missed
his supper.
Supper's over,
the dishes are clean,
And there's nothing left
but one old bean.

Silly Slim Slupper
was a funny man.
He washed his feet
in a coffee can.
He wore a pot
upon his head
And slept on a horse
instead of a bed.

(continued)

Stay out of the way
   of Silly Slim Slupper
Mad because he missed
   his supper.
Supper's over,
   the dishes are clean,
And there's nothing left
   but one old bean.

[handwritten: chorus etc. ↓]

Silly Slim Slupper
   bought an old farm.
He put the cows in the house
   and kids in the barn.
He dressed the cows
   in new silk gowns
And dressed his kids
   in hand-me-downs.

[handwritten: Point it out]

Stay out of the way
   of Silly Slim Slupper
Mad because he missed
   his supper.
Supper's over,
   the dishes are clean,
And there's nothing left
   but one old bean.

Now, Silly Slim Slupper
   is old and gray,
And all his neighbors
   have moved away.
But he still lives
   out on his farm,
With cows in the house
   and kids in the barn.

Stay out of the way
   of Silly Slim Slupper
Mad because he missed
   his supper.
Supper's over,
   the dishes are clean,
And there's nothing left
   but one old bean.

by Maurice Poe

[handwritten: Ask:]

What was the oddest thing Slim Slupper did? How is his behavior different from what you would do?

I'm going to read the poem again. This time I want you to join me in chanting (singing) the chorus. Read or sing the poem a second time. *[handwritten: Do slow the first time so til they got the chorus.]* Turn to page 66 in your book. Look at the picture of Silly Slim Slupper. What is he doing? Look at the picture on page 67. Why is the cow dressed that way? Now, turn to the picture of Silly Slim Slupper on page 68. Why does he look that way? How do you think he feels?

Look at the part of the poem that describes the way Silly Slim Slupper treated his cows and his kids. Do you find this treatment unusual? Why or why not? What are "hand-me-downs"? How do you think his kids feel about living in a barn? What would be some disadvantages of living in a barn? Would there be any advantages?

Now, let's read the poem together. Lead the students in a lively group reading. *[handwritten: Try to keep the tempo going!]*

After reading this poem several times, I keep wondering why Silly Slim Slupper is always late for his supper. Why do you think he is always late for supper? Let's share our ideas, and I'll write them on the chalkboard. Let's see how many ideas we can think up. On the chalkboard, write the students' responses. *[handwritten: — briefly]*

You've come up with some great ideas about why he might be late for supper. The poem says to "stay out of the way of Silly Slim Slupper." Why do you think we're told to get out of his way? What kind of a mood would you be in if you missed supper?

Putting Ideas to Work

Things to Talk About

Materials
- Page 69 in student book
- Chalkboard and chalk

Look at page 69 in your book. "Things to Talk About" asks us to do some thinking about Silly Slim Slupper.

Read number 1 with me. "What is the *most* ridiculous thing that happens in this rhyme?" Silly Slim Slupper does a lot of ridiculous things. What do you think is the *most* ridiculous thing he does?

Some possible student responses
a. He brushed his teeth with a piece of steel.
b. He wore a pot upon his head.
c. He dressed the cows in new silk gowns.

Read number 2 with me. "What would be the advantages and disadvantages in having Silly Slim Slupper as a neighbor?" On the chalkboard, write *Advantages* and *Disadvantages*. List the students' responses under the appropriate heading.

Some possible student responses
Advantages —
a. His neighbors find him entertaining.
b. He gives his neighbors something to talk about.
Disadvantages —
a. The neighbors don't like to visit because the cows live in the house.
b. The neighborhood children are afraid of him.

Read number 3 with me. "How would you describe Silly Slim Slupper to someone who had never met him before?" This poem tells us quite a bit about Silly Slim Slupper so it shouldn't be too difficult to describe him. I'll list your ideas on the chalkboard. Have the students describe Silly Slim Slupper. Write their descriptions on the chalkboard.

Collect copies poem.

Read number 4 with me. "What makes this poem a real tongue twister? Do you know any other tongue twisters? Share them with the class." I'm sure you've heard lots of tongue twisters. That's when you say a bunch of words quickly, and your tongue doesn't seem to work just right. The name "Silly Slim Slupper" is an example of a tongue twister. Try to say that three times fast! What other tongue twisters do you know? Have the students share other familiar tongue twisters.

Things to Do

Materials
- Page 69 in student book
- Writing paper
- Pencils

Look at the "Things to Do" on page 69 in your book. Ask each student to choose one of two the three activities to do, or pick one for the whole class to do.

Let's read number 1 together. "Make a list of *other* silly things Silly Slim Slupper might do." From the sound of this poem, Silly Slim Slupper is a man who is *always* doing silly things. Think of some silly things he might do that are *not* mentioned in the poem. Have the students list silly things Silly Slim Slupper might do.

Let's read number 2 together. "Write a short story that tells why all of Silly Slim Slupper's neighbors moved away." Have the students write stories about Silly Slim Slupper's neighbors.

Let's read number 3 together. "Was there ever a time when you missed supper? Why? Write about what happened." Have the students write about times when they missed supper.

As kids start to finish, they can share their writing in front of the class using the karaoke machine.

Extending Language and Thinking

Activity

Objectives
- to produce examples of alliteration
- to illustrate examples of alliteration

Materials
- Chalkboard and chalk
- Drawing paper
- Crayons

This poem lends itself to the study of alliteration. Share the idea that sometimes writers try to make their ideas more colorful and fun to read by using words that begin with the same sound. On the chalkboard, write *Silly Slim Slupper* and point out that the poet used the same beginning sound to make this character's name sound unusual or funny.

On the chalkboard, write the word *snakes*. Ask the students to think of words that begin with the letter *s* and that could be used to describe snakes. (For example, *small, slimy, slithery, sneaky,* etc.) After several words have been suggested, combine the words to form a descriptive phrase. (For example, *small slithery snakes.*)

Lead the class in brainstorming action words that begin with the letter *s* to add to the phrase. (For example, *sneak, sing, slide,* etc.) After several words have been suggested, combine the words to form a sentence. (For example, *Small slithery snakes sing.*)

On the chalkboard, write a list of common nouns. (For example, *frog, baby, dog, tree, spider,* etc.) Encourage the students to think of words they could put together to form some alliterative phrases. (For example, *five fat furry frogs.*)

As a follow-up activity, have the students illustrate one of the phrases.

Strengthening Language for Second-Language Learners

Activity

Objectives
- to promote auditory discrimination
- to reinforce sight-word recognition
- to foster memory recall

Materials
- Chalkboard and chalk
- Index cards
- Markers

On the chalkboard, print the words *frying, pan, comb, hair, washed, can, teeth, clean, dishes, house,* and *barn.* Then, ask the students to print each word on an index card. Have the students arrange their cards on top of their desks.

We're going to play a game called "Find My Word." Each sentence I read will contain one of the words you've printed on your word cards. Listen carefully as I read each sentence. When you hear the word, put your finger on that word card. The second time I read the sentence hold up the word card when you hear me read the word. After I finish reading the sentence a second time, I want you to repeat the sentence aloud. Read each sentence slowly and deliberately. If the students have difficulty identifying the correct word, read the sentence again with an emphasis on the target word. Model the process for the students.

Teacher:
My room is *clean*. (Each student points to the word *clean* on his word card.)

My room is *clean*. (Each student holds up his word card.)

Student:
My room is *clean*.

Continue this pattern with the following sentences.

1. **She is cooking eggs in the *pan*.**
2. **Do you have my *comb*?**
3. **He is *frying* bacon.**
4. **Her *hair* is brown.**

5. He *washed* his hands.
6. Her *teeth* are nice and white.
7. She came to my *house*.
8. Put the *dishes* on the table.
9. He bought a *can* of green beans.
10. We put hay in the *barn*.

Reaching Across the Curriculum

Expanding Literature

Activity

Objective
- to share a children's poetry book

Material
- Children's book
  Prelutsky, Jack. *A Gopher in the Garden and Other Animal Poems*. New York: The Macmillan Company, 1967.

Share *A Gopher in the Garden and Other Animal Poems* written by Jack Prelutsky. This is a marvelous collection of rollicking, tongue-twisting rhymes about animals of all kinds. The illustrations are humorous and provide a perfect accompaniment to the verses. This is an excellent book to share with the students prior to engaging them in writing and illustrating their own tongue-twisting alliterative verses as suggested in the following activity.

Developing Creative Expression

Activity

Objectives
- to produce other examples of alliteration
- to illustrate examples of alliteration

Materials
- Chalkboard and chalk
- Writing paper
- Pencils
- Drawing paper
- Crayons
- Bulletin board

Read the following alliterative sentences to the students.

Brave bugs bite brown bulls.
Daring donkeys dig for daisies in the dusty ditch.

On the chalkboard, write the following words.

Bold baboons	*Kindly kangaroos*
Giant giraffes	*Gold gophers*
Marvelous monkeys	*Lazy lions*
Dangerous dogs	*Caring cats*

Divide the students into small groups. Have each group choose one of the sets of words. Let them brainstorm words that begin with the same first letter as the words in the set. Once lists of words have been generated, have the students write alliterative sentences about their characters. Then, have the students illustrate their sentences. Post sentences and illustrations on a bulletin board.

McDenter, the Bad News Inventor

His repeated failures do not seem to discourage young Harvey McDenter, the Bad News Inventor. However, he may run into trouble finding willing candidates to try out his unusual inventions. The consequences of Harvey's experiments will tickle your students as they read and react to one disaster after another.

Objectives:

Students will
- identify character traits.
- practice choral/oral reading.
- make predictions based on known information.
- extend language and ideas through oral and written expression.

Warming Up for Reading

Materials
- Chalkboard and chalk

On the chalkboard, write the word *inventor*.

What are the names of some famous inventors that you've heard or read about? List the students' responses on the chalkboard.

What qualities or characteristics do you think an inventor needs? What problems do you think an inventor might have?

Today, you're going to meet a young inventor who runs into trouble with his inventions. Our poem introduces Harvey McDenter, a *novice* inventor.

On the chalkboard, write the word *novice*. **What do you think the word *novice* means?** Accept the students' responses, clarifying that a *novice* is a *beginner*.

As I read the poem, listen to discover some of the problems that young Harvey encounters.

Sharing the Poem

Materials
- Pages 70-71 in student book
- Chalkboard and chalk

Read the poem expressively, pausing to shake your head after reading about the awful consequences of each of Harvey's inventions.

McDenter, the Bad News Inventor

Young Harvey McDenter,
    a novice inventor,
    sure started a hullabaloo
By concocting a potion,
    a milk-colored lotion.
    He called it "McDenter Shampoo."

He gave it to Sue,
    a girl that he knew,
    when he saw her one day at the mall.
Sue shampooed with the potion,
    a milk-colored lotion,
    which made her as bald as a ball!

Young Harvey McDenter,
    a novice inventor,
    developed a thinking machine,
A helmet with wires
    and sparks that shot fires
    and antenna that looked real mean.

(continued)

He bribed young brother Ned
   to try it on his head
     with the promise that it wouldn't harm.
The machine spit out smoke,
   as Ned started to choke,
     and the neighbors turned in an alarm.

Young Harvey McDenter,
   a novice inventor,
     created a robot one day.
Thought it could do chores —
   wash windows and doors.
     He smiled as he went on his way.

The robot crept up,
   while Mom held a cup
     of hot steaming coffee in her hand.
She shrieked her distress,
   made a mess of her dress.
     It wasn't what Harvey had planned!

Young Harvey McDenter,
   no more an inventor,
     has been threatened with all kinds of pain.
But his aunt in Tibet
   sent a chemistry set.
     You can **bet** he'll be at it again!

by Barbara Schmidt and Maurice Poe

What were the three inventions that Harvey created? On the chalkboard, list the inventions.

How successful were his inventions? Who were the three unlucky guinea pigs that Harvey chose to use for his experiments? Do you think Harvey's inventing career is over? Why? Why not?

Turn to page 70 in your book. Look at the picture. **What's happening to poor Sue? Which of Harvey's inventions do you see in the picture on page 71? Why is the coffee cup sailing through the air?**

[handwritten margin note: Pass it out.]

Let's look for some unique words in the first stanza of the poem. Find the word that means a *big commotion.* (hullabaloo) *[handwritten: uproar]*
Which word means *preparing?* (concocting)
Which word means a *liquid?* (potion)

Let's read the poem together a few times. Try to capture the rhythm of the poem. Coach the students through several readings. *[handwritten: All read in unison. Remind students to speak as if we're all 1. voice.]*

Now, we need three students to act out the roles of the unfortunate victims of Harvey's inventions. Select three students to portray the characters Sue, Ned, and Mom. **We'll stop the poem after Harvey tries out one of his inventions so that each victim can scold Harvey. Tell him how you feel about what has happened.** Have the whole class read the poem aloud pausing for reactions from Sue, Ned, and Mom. *[handwritten: But be polite!]*

[handwritten: Repeat. Have rows read each stanza instead of whole class.]

Putting Ideas to Work

Things to Talk About

Materials
- Page 72 in student book
- Chalkboard and chalk *[handwritten: handout.]*

Look at page 72 in your book. *[handwritten: handout]* **"Things to Talk About" asks us to do some thinking about Harvey and his inventions.**

Read the first question with me. "What words would you use to describe Harvey to someone who doesn't know him?" List the students' responses on the chalkboard.

Some possible student responses — crazy, unlucky, creative

Read the second question with me. "Why does Harvey deserve to be called 'the Bad News Inventor'?" Discuss with the students what is meant by "Bad News."

Possible student response — Any time he invents something, it means "bad news" for whoever uses it.

Read the third set of questions with me. "Would you be willing to try out one of Harvey's inventions? Why? Why not?" I doubt *any* of you would be willing to try one of the "bad news" inventions described in the poem! Suppose Harvey invented something new and interesting. Would you try out his new invention for him?

Some possible student responses
a. Yes, Harvey's luck might change.
b. No, I wouldn't trust anything *he* makes.

Read the fourth set of questions with me. "Which of Harvey's inventions do you think is the most imaginative? Which is the most useful?"

Some possible student responses
Imaginative — the thinking machine
Useful — the robot

Things To Do

Materials
- Page 72 in student book
- Writing paper
- Pencils
- Drawing paper
- Crayons

Look at the "Things to Do" on page 72 in your book. Ask each student to choose one of the three activities to do, or pick one for the whole class to do.

handout

Teacher reads each one first.

Let's read number 1 together. "What do you predict Harvey will try to create with the chemistry set? What will be the results? Describe what Harvey will try to create and draw a picture of it." Have the students write about and illustrate Harvey's next creation.

Let's read number 2 together. "The poem says that Harvey was 'threatened with all kinds of pain.' Write the conversation that you think took place between Harvey and his mother following the robot incident. What kinds of threats do you think his mom made?" Have the students write the dialogue for a conversation between Harvey and his mother.

Remind students to put name and number of activity they are doing.

Let's read number 3 together. "Be Harvey McDenter for a day. Think up a possible no-win invention. Draw your invention and label the parts or ingredients." Have the students create and illustrate a new Harvey McDenter invention.

Have kids start work with 5 minutes of thinking silence. After 15 or 20 minutes they (volunteers) can share in front of the class. Lots will volunteer!

Extending Language and Thinking

Activity 1

Objective
- to identify cause and effect relationships

Materials
- Chalkboard and chalk
- Writing paper
- Pencils

On the chalkboard, draw two columns. At the top of the first column, write *Cause* and at the top of the second column, write *Effect.* Underneath *Cause,* write *McDenter Shampoo.*

We've talked before about cause and effect relationships. An event or incident can be the *cause* of something that happens. What happens is the *effect*. There were some pretty unusual effects that took place in this poem. For example, what effect did McDenter Shampoo have on poor Sue? Under the *Effect* column on the chalkboard, write *made her as bald as a ball.* Then, have the students identify the two other cause and effect relationships in the poem. Write their responses under the appropriate columns on the chalkboard.

In the poem, Harvey's inventions had some unfortunate effects. What if Harvey's inventions had *worked*? What if his experiments had been successful? Dramatically erase the information in the *Effect* column.

1 & 3 - white jar - on table

1 & 2 - box, bookshelf

Let's pretend Harvey's inventions had worked. On your paper, make two columns as I did on the chalkboard. Under *Cause,* list Harvey's three inventions. Under *Effect,* come up with your own versions of successful results. When you're through, we'll share and compare your ideas. I'm sure Harvey would be delighted with your results! Have the students complete their lists. Then, discuss their results.

Activity 2

Objective
- to reinforce understanding of suffixes

Materials
- Chalkboard and chalk
- Writing paper
- Pencils

This selection offers a good opportunity to reinforce the students' understanding of suffixes.

On the chalkboard, write the following.

Process	One Who Performs Process	Product
invent	inventor	invention

Using the material on the chalkboard as a model, guide a class discussion about the many possibilities for adding different endings to root words.

Add the following words to the list on the chalkboard.

create	creator	creation
explore	explorer	exploration
navigate	navigator	navigation

Discuss the meaning of these words. Point out how some words drop the final *e* before adding a suffix.

Encourage the students to develop their own lists of words based on the samples on the chalkboard.

Strengthening Language for Second-Language Learners

Activity 1

Objective
- to recognize past tense forms of verbs that add *ed* or *d*

Materials
- Chalkboard and chalk
- Pages 70-71 in student book
- Writing paper
- Pencils

There are several verbs in the poem that form the past tense by adding *ed* or *d* to their present forms. For example, the words *started, called, created,* and *shampooed* all refer to action that took place in the past.

To illustrate this grammatical rule, conduct the following activity. First, ask a student to perform an action such as jumping, hopping, or talking. Then, stop the student. After the student has stopped performing the action, write a sentence on the chalkboard similar to the following.

_____ *jumped.*
(Student's name)   (verb for the action performed)

Underline the *ed* in the verb. Explain that the student's action is over or past and that one way of showing this is by adding *ed* or *d* to the end of the verb. Tell the student that it is sometimes necessary to double the ending consonant of a verb with a short vowel before adding the *ed* ending.

Then, have the student repeat the same action. Do not stop her this time. While the action is still going on, write the following sentence on the chalkboard.

_____ *jumps.*
(Student's name)   (verb for the action)

Explain that the student is performing the action right now.

Point out that many words in "McDenter, the Bad News Inventor" show action that has taken place in the past. Have the students locate and list the action words in the poem that have the *ed* ending.

Activity 2

Objectives
- to identify describing words in the poem
- to practice using describing words

Materials
- Chalkboard and chalk
- A familiar object
- Writing paper
- Pencils

Point out to the students how the poet used descriptive words to help the reader *see* each of Harvey's inventions. Have the students find some describing words in the poem. Write these descriptive words on the chalkboard. Explain that describing what things look like and what they do is important for a writer.

Display a familiar object such as a popcorn popper, a globe, or a tape recorder. Have the students write descriptions of the object explaining what the object looks like and what it does.

Reaching Across the Curriculum

Developing Creative Expression

Activity

Objective
- to develop newspaper advertisements

Materials
- Writing paper
- Pencils

Have the students develop newspaper advertisements for one of Harvey's inventions. Have the students describe the advantages of owning the invention. The advertisements should also include the price, the size, and a detailed description of the invention.

Expanding Social Studies

Activity 1

Objectives
- to read biographies of inventors
- to create news articles

Materials
- Biographies of famous inventors
- Writing paper
- Pencils

Have the students locate and read biographies of famous inventors. Let them share the information they've learned by writing news articles about one of the inventions. Tell the students to include information about the inventor and the invention and how it has affected people's lives. Have them also tell where and when the invention took place.

Activity 2

Objective
- to identify important inventions

Materials
- Writing paper
- Pencils
- Library sources

Have the students work in small groups to brainstorm five inventions that they consider the most important. Have them rank these inventions in order of their importance. Give the students opportunities to share their lists and to explain why they consider these inventions important.

As a follow-up assignment, have the students conduct research about the individuals who were responsible for the inventions that they've listed.

Lesson 25

Padoodle, Padiddle

There's a method to the madness of the nonsensical language in this poem. See how quickly your students catch on to the *riddle in the middle* of each rhyme. The secret is that each word has double letters in it.

Objectives:

Students will
- analyze strategies for solving riddles.
- practice choral/oral reading.
- create new riddles.
- extend language and ideas through oral and written expression.

Warming Up for Reading

Materials
- Chalkboard and chalk

Heard any good riddles lately? See if you can figure this one out. What's black and white and red all over? It *could* be a sunburned zebra! What if *red* is spelled R-E-A-D? Then, the answer is *a newspaper!* That riddle is older than I am! I know how much you like hearing riddles and jokes! Why *do* you think people like riddles and jokes so much?

How do you go about trying to figure out the answer to a riddle? Accept the students' responses encouraging them to discuss the importance of clues.

I have a feeling that you're going to catch on quickly to the riddles in the poem you're about to hear. There's even a good clue in the title. On the chalkboard, write *Padoodle, Padiddle.* **Examine the title carefully as you listen.**

Sharing the Poem

Material
- Page 73 in student book

Read the poem expressively, pointing to the title on the chalkboard every time the chorus is read.

Padoodle, Padiddle

Padoodle, padiddle, I'll give you a riddle.
  And if you can guess it, it's yours!

Tallahassee, Kalamazoo,
Throw in *Chattanooga,* too.
Riddle some up. Riddle some down.
What's alike about each town?

Padoodle, padiddle, I'll give you a riddle.
  And if you can guess it, it's yours!

Larry, Barry, but not Gary.
Sally, Allie, but not Mary.
Padoodle the riddle to this game.
It's not easy. Who's to blame?

Padoodle, padiddle, I'll give you a riddle.
  And if you can guess it, it's yours!

Butter's better, so's an *apple.*
Spaghetti, lettuce, even *scrapple.*
Riddle some foods, like a *burrito.*
What's alike about each treato?

Padoodle, padiddle, I'll give you a riddle.
  And if you can guess it, it's yours!

Big is not as good as *little.*
Not the outside, but the *middle.*
Not a banjo, but a *fiddle.*
Padoodle, padiddle, guess the riddle!

  by Barbara Schmidt

Raise your hand if you think you've figured out the riddle, *but don't give it away!* Maybe you need more time to think about it. Looking at the poem may help. Turn to page 73 in your book. Look at the picture. Does this girl know the answer to the riddle? I'll read the stanzas while you follow along with your eyes. Join in when I read the chorus. Guide the students through the poem.

Okay, riddlers, tell me what's alike about the towns in the second stanza. Accept the students' responses. Tell them to carefully examine the names of the towns. Help them realize that they all contain *double letters.*

Well, that gives it away! Did anyone figure out the riddle before now? How were you able to figure it out?

Take a look at the fourth stanza. Why *Larry* and *Barry* but not *Gary?* Why *Sally* and *Allie* but not *Mary?* Yes, those words have double letters!

How about the foods in the sixth stanza? Were you able to figure out that all the foods have double letters, too? How about the words in the last stanza? *Little, middle,* and *fiddle* all contain double letters, don't they?

Now, it's time for a group reading! Divide the class into four groups. Assign each group one stanza to read aloud. The whole class should read the chorus.

Putting Ideas to Work

Things to Talk About

Material
● Page 74 in student book

Look at page 74 in your book. "Things to Talk About" asks us to do some thinking about riddles.

Read number 1 with me. "How did you figure out the riddle? What helped you?" Have the students tell how they figured out the riddle.

Read number 2 with me. "Why do you think the poet chose 'Padoodle, Padiddle' as the title of this rhyme?" "Padoodle, Padiddle" is a pretty strange name for a poem! Why do you suppose the poet chose it?

Possible student response — Both words contain double letters.

Read number 3 with me. "What's a good riddle you've heard? Share it." Have the students share riddles.

Read number 4 with me. "Why do people like riddles and jokes?"

Some possible student responses
a. They're funny.
b. They're fun to try to figure out.
c. They make you think.

Things to Do

Materials
● Pages 73-74 in student book
● Writing paper
● Pencils

Look at the "Things to Do" on page 74 in your book. Ask each student to choose one of the three activities to do, or pick one for the whole class to do.

Let's read number 1 together. "Think of one new riddle word for each stanza. You will need the name of a town or city, the name of a person, the name of a food, and the name of a word for a word association. Make sure the words you choose fit the riddle pattern." Have the students think of a new riddle word for each stanza. Remind them that their words should all contain double letters.

Let's read number 2 together. "Make up your own 'Padoodle, Padiddle' stanza for the poem. Use kinds of clothes, sports, or animals whose names fit the riddle pattern." Write the fourth stanza of the poem on your paper leaving out the names Larry, Barry, Gary, Sally, Allie, and Mary. Then, fill in the blanks with new words. All of your words should be the same kind of thing, for instance clothes, sports, or animals. Remember, the first two blanks in each line should be filled in with words **with** double letters. The last blank in each line should contain a word *without* double letters. Have the students make up new versions of the fourth stanza of the poem.

Let's read number 3 together. "Share the poem with someone who has never heard it before. See if the person can figure out how the riddle words in each stanza are alike." Have the students share the poem with others.

Extending Language and Thinking

Activity 1

Objectives
- to play a riddle game
- to classify and categorize information

Materials
- Chalkboard and chalk

Here's another riddle game! Maybe you've played it before. I call it "Aunt Tillie likes . . ." To figure out the riddle, you have to listen very carefully to the names of the things that Aunt Tillie likes and the names of things that she doesn't like. Here we go.

Aunt Tillie likes *bread,* but she doesn't like *muffins.*
Aunt Tillie likes *breakfast,* but she doesn't like *lunch.*
Aunt Tillie likes *brooms,* but she doesn't like *mops.*

Now, tell me some other things Aunt Tillie likes. Have the students suggest names of other things Aunt Tillie likes. If a student suggests something that begins with the *br* blend, write it on the chalkboard. If a student's suggestion doesn't begin with the *br* blend, say **No, Aunt Tillie doesn't like that/those.**

Continue the "Aunt Tillie likes . . ." game using the following clues.

For *Opposites*
Aunt Tillie likes going *upstairs,* but she doesn't like going *downstairs.*
Aunt Tillie likes *night,* but she doesn't like *day.*

For *Categories*
Aunt Tillie likes *soccer,* but she doesn't like *knitting.*
Aunt Tillie likes *baseball,* but she doesn't like *shopping.*

For *Words Ending in tion*
Aunt Tillie likes *vacations,* but she doesn't like *traveling.*
Aunt Tillie likes *inventions,* but she doesn't like *cars.*

As an extension, have the students make up their own "Aunt Tillie likes . . ." riddles.

Activity 2

Objective
- to practice classifying

Materials
- Duplicating master
- Pencils

The riddle words in "Padoodle, Padiddle" fit into the four categories of towns, names, foods, and word associations. For the students who need practice in grouping and classifying, copy the following on a duplicating master for the students.

	Sports	Foods	Cities	Animals	Clothing
P	polo				
L		lettuce			
A			Albany		
Y				yak	
S					sweater

For each category, explain to the students that they must try to think of a word that begins with each letter on the left side of the paper. Have the students work in pairs to complete the chart. Tell the students that they may not be able to fill in all the boxes.

Strengthening Language for Second-Language Learners

Activity 1

Objective
- to create riddles

Material
- None

Encourage the students to make up simple riddles based on the following models.

I am the color of grass, a frog, and a traffic light that means *go*. What color am I?

I am something used to write with. I am usually white, and I can make a squeaky noise on the chalkboard. What am I?

Activity 2

Objective
- to practice word association

Materials
- Chalkboard and chalk

On the chalkboard, write the words *arm, leg, dog,* and *hand.* Ask the students to identify the word that doesn't belong with the others. Have them explain why they made their choice. Then, encourage the students to suggest more words that *do* belong with the others. Continue this activity using other categories of words.

Reaching Across the Curriculum

Developing Creative Expression

Activity

Objective
- to produce a class riddle book

Materials
- Writing paper
- Pencils
- Construction paper
- Markers

Publish a class *"Padoodle, Padiddle" Riddle Book.* Have each student carefully copy a favorite riddle onto paper. When the individual pages are complete, have the students work together to create a cover, a title page, a page of acknowledgments, and a table of contents. If possible, duplicate the book and give each student a copy.

Exploring Science and Social Studies

Activity

Objective
- to create riddles about facts

Materials
- Writing paper
- Pencils

Have the students make up riddles about facts they've read about in their science or social studies textbooks. A riddle about rainbows might be similar to the following.

It appears in the sky after a rainstorm.
The colors form a beautiful half circle in the sky.

Expanding Literature

Activity

Objective
- to share favorite riddles

Materials
- Books of riddles
- Construction paper
- Markers
- Bulletin board

Create a "Padoodle, Padiddle" bulletin board display. Have the students read books of riddles. Ask them to select their favorite riddles and let them write the riddles on colorful construction paper for display on the bulletin board.

Lesson 26

Guess Who Doesn't Have a Hobby?

Your students will empathize with this sad lament of a student overwhelmed by the achievements of classmates! While it's okay *not* to have a hobby, this selection will provide opportunities for your students to focus on making creative choices about how to spend their spare time.

Objectives:

Students will
- share personal experiences related to the theme of the poem.
- practice choral/oral reading.
- classify information.
- extend language and ideas through oral and written expression.

Warming Up for Reading

Materials
- Chalkboard and chalk
- Writing paper
- Pencils

On the chalkboard, write the following.

List any hobbies that you have.

Someday you may have to fill out a job application or an application for college. When you do, you may come across a request like the one I've written on the chalkboard. The application may ask you to list your hobbies. Why do you think anyone would ask you to do that? Accept the students' responses. Discuss how someone can get to know you better by knowing about your interests and talents.

How would you fill in the request on the chalkboard? Take a few minutes to think about what you do in your spare time. Write a list. Provide adequate time for the students to think and respond.

On the chalkboard, draw the following diagram.

What are some things you like to do in your spare time? I'll write them on the spokes of this "hobby wheel." Write the students' responses on the chalkboard. Lead a class discussion about the students' various interests and talents.

Why do you think people have hobbies? What if someone asked you to list your hobbies and you didn't have any? How would you feel? That's how the poet in today's poem feels! What a dilemma! As I read the poem, listen to see if the problem is solved.

Sharing the Poem

Materials
- Pages 75-76 in student book

Read the poem in an expressive, plaintive voice. Encourage the students to join in on the chorus.

(Turn the page for the poem.)

Guess Who Doesn't Have a Hobby?

Jamie's into baseball;
   he really knows the score.
Has three-hundred baseball cards,
   maybe even more.
Mark is a computer hack,
   spends hours at the screen.
Julie's got a stamp collection
   like you've never seen.

Guess who doesn't have a hobby?

Sue is our class shutter bug;
   she even won a prize.
And David's acrobatics
   would make you roll your eyes.
Jo-Jo runs in marathons;
   the kids line up to root.
And Amy can make stained glass,
   and Gina plays the flute.

Guess who doesn't have a hobby?

Angie, she can lip-sync
   to any song she hears.
And how about the magic tricks
   that Andy volunteers?
Did I mention Becky's ballet?
   Kim Lee's homemade cake?
Or the antique model ships
   that Jeff and Brian make?

Guess who doesn't have a hobby?

Every year on Hobby Day,
   we share what we can do.
And there I was — no hobby!
   How embarrassing! How true!
The teacher said, "It's your turn.
   Tell us how you spend your time."
I blushed and then I stammered,
   "What I do . . . I guess . . . is **rhyme!**"

Guess who finally came up with a hobby!

by Barbara Schmidt

What was the poet's problem in the poem? How did the poet feel about the problem? Was there a solution? What was it? Did the solution surprise you?

Look at *our* list of hobbies on the chalkboard. Do the children in the poem have any of the same hobbies we do? David's hobby was acrobatics. Do you know what that is? Jo-Jo's hobby is running in marathons. What's a marathon?

Turn to page 75 in your book. Look at the picture. What's the hobby of the girl in the picture? Can you find her name in the poem on this page? Turn to page 76. What's the hobby of the boy in the picture? Can you find his name in the poem on this page? Turn back to page 75. Let's read the poem together. Guide the students through several readings. Encourage them to sound sad when they read the chorus, except when they come to the last chorus. For this chorus, tell them to make their voices sound excited and happy.

Since this poem sounds like it could take place right here in our classroom, let's do a "Readers' Theater." Select individual students to read about each of the students in the poem. Each student should stand in the front of the room with her back to the audience. As the poem is presented, each student should turn around and read her part when it's time.

For a variation, substitute the names of students in the class for the names in the poem. For another variation, have one student read the entire poem aloud while individual students pantomime the hobbies mentioned in the poem.

Putting Ideas to Work

Things to Talk About

Materials
- Page 77 in student book
- Chalkboard and chalk

Look at page 77 in your book. "Things to Talk About" asks us to do some thinking about hobbies.

Read the first question with me. "Which of the hobbies in the poem do you wish you could do?" List the students' responses on the chalkboard.

Some possible student responses — computers, magic tricks, ballet

Read the second set of questions with me. "How did the poet feel about not having a hobby? How do you know?"

Possible student responses — embarrassed, jealous. She kept saying, "Guess who doesn't have a hobby?"

Read number 3 with me. "What are some advantages of having a hobby? What might be a disadvantage of having a hobby?" Have the students name the advantages of having a hobby and at least one disadvantage.

Some possible student responses
Advantages —
a. You have a fun way to spend free time.
b. You can learn something new.

Disadvantage —
   You might want to spend all your time on your hobby instead of doing the things you need to do.

Read the fourth question with me. "How do you think the other students reacted to the poet's hobby?" The poet's hobby is a little unusual. How do you think the other students felt about it?

Some possible student responses
a. They thought it was boring.
b. They thought it was neat and wanted the poet to make up more rhymes about the class.
c. They thought it was silly.

Things to Do

Materials
- Page 77 in student book
- Writing paper
- Pencils

Look at the "Things to Do" on page 77 in your book. Ask each student to choose one of the three activities to do, or pick one for the whole class to do.

Let's read number 1 together. "Make a list of the things you like to do in your spare time. Which of these things do you consider a *hobby?* Explain why." First, make a list of things you do in your spare time. Choose one that you would consider a hobby and put a check mark beside it. Then, below the list, write about the hobby that you've checked off. Have each student make a list of leisure activities and write about one that's a hobby.

Let's read number 2 together. "Make a list of hobbies that are not mentioned in the poem. See how many you can list." Have the students make lists of hobbies.

Let's read number 3 together. "Think up a way to divide the hobbies mentioned in the poem into two groups. For example, you might group them according to *things to do inside* and *things to do outside*. Once you have figured out how you want to group the hobbies, fold a piece of paper in half the long way. Decide on the title for each group. Write a title at the top of each column. List the appropriate hobbies under each title. Some hobbies might be listed under both titles." Have the students categorize the hobbies mentioned in the poem.

Extending Language and Thinking

Activity

Objectives
- to hold a "Hobby Day"
- to improve oral communication skills
- to practice organizing thoughts and language

Materials
- Chalkboard and chalk

By now, we've talked a little bit about our interests, the special things we like to do when we're not at school. I bet you don't consider some of these interests *hobbies,* but they really are. After all, a hobby is simply something enjoyable that someone does in her spare time.

Do you remember the "Hobby Day" that took place in the poem? Well, this week we're going to try the same thing in our room. There *will* be one big difference, though. Instead of just *telling* us about your special interest, you're going to *teach* us a little about what you like to do. Just as I need to prepare for what I try to teach you every day, you'll need to prepare to teach us about your special interest. For example, suppose *(a student's name)* wanted to teach us about *(student's hobby)*. How would she go about planning the lesson? Guide the students in a discussion. Be sure to discuss ways to capture the audience's interest, ways that objects and demonstrations can add to the presentation, and ways to involve the class in the lesson. List the students' suggestions on the chalkboard.

Set aside time for the students' presentations. This activity will give the students opportunities to improve oral communication skills and to practice organizing thoughts and language.

Strengthening Language for Second-Language Learners

Activity

Objective
- to identify good leisure activities

Materials
- Chalkboard and chalk
- Writing paper
- Pencils

On the chalkboard, write the following. *When I'm not in school, I like to _____ .* Encourage the students to orally complete this sentence. Then, write the following sentence frames on the chalkboard for the students to complete, either aloud or in writing.

I like to _____ on rainy days.
I like to _____ on sunny days.
I like to _____ in the afternoon.
I like to _____ before I go to bed.
I like to _____ by myself.
I like to _____ with a friend.

Reaching Across the Curriculum
Expanding Social Studies
Activity 1

Objective
- to interview people about hobbies

Materials
- Writing paper
- Pencils

Survey your friends and family about favorite hobbies. Interview them to find out how they chose their hobbies and what they think the benefits of their hobbies are. Encourage the students to come up with a variety of questions for their interviews. Have them share their findings.

Activity 2

Objectives
- to discuss benefits of hobbies
- to keep a log of leisure activities
- to evaluate leisure activities

Materials
- Writing paper
- Pencils

With the students, discuss the benefits of hobbies and how hobbies can provide valuable experiences for future endeavors. Discuss the concept of planning for leisure activities. Have the students keep a log to record what they do in their spare time. Then, discuss the results of the log. Encourage the students to evaluate the personal usefulness of their leisure activities.

Activity 3

Objective
* to research a new hobby

Materials
* Library sources
* Writing paper
* Pencils

Select a hobby that you would like to try. Find out as much as you can about this hobby. Then, write about it. Tell what the hobby is, what it involves, and why you would like to try it.

Activity 4

Objective
* to research unusual hobbies

Materials
* Library sources
* Writing paper
* Pencils

Have the students locate information about unusual pastimes and hobbies. The *Guinness Book of World Records* may be a particularly good source. Have the students present brief oral reports on their findings.

I Found a Four-Leaf Clover

In Jack Prelutsky's tale of woe, four-leaf clovers aren't all they're cracked up to be! The mishaps the poet encounters should amuse your students and lead to a discussion about superstitions.

Objectives:

Students will

- share personal experiences.
- think critically by analyzing characteristics of superstitions.
- practice choral/oral reading.
- utilize creative writing abilities.
- extend language and ideas through oral and written expression.

Warming Up for Reading

Materials

- Chalkboard and chalk

On the chalkboard, write the word *superstition.*

Imagine that these three things happened to you on your way to school today. First, a black cat ran across your path. Next, you had to walk under a ladder where some painters were painting a house. Then, you stepped on a crack in the sidewalk. If you believed in superstitions, how would you feel about the things that happened? Why would you feel that way?

Explain that superstitions are beliefs that people have made up to explain why things happen. Many superstitions are hundreds of years old. They are not based on facts and cannot be proven.

Would you *really* have bad luck if you walked under a ladder or stepped on a crack? Why? Why not? Have you heard of any other superstitions? What are they?

Have you ever heard of the superstition about finding a four-leaf clover? If *you* were superstitious, what would you expect to happen if you found a four-leaf clover? If necessary, explain that four-leaf clovers are supposed to be signs of good luck.

Today's poem is about someone who finds a four-leaf clover. What happens after he finds it may surprise you! As I read the poem, listen to how the character's experiences cause him to change his mind about four-leaf clovers.

Sharing the Poem

Materials

- Chalkboard and chalk
- Pages 78-79 in student book

Read the poem expressively to the students.

I Found a Four-Leaf Clover

I found a four-leaf clover
and was happy with my find,
but with time to think it over,
I've entirely changed my mind.
I concealed it in my pocket,
safe inside a paper pad,
soon, much swifter than a rocket,
my good fortune turned to bad.

(continued)

I smashed my fingers in a door,
I dropped a dozen eggs,
I slipped and tumbled to the floor,
a dog nipped both my legs,
my ring slid down the bathtub drain,
my pen leaked on my shirt,
I barked my shin, I missed my train,
I sat on my dessert.

I broke my brand-new glasses,
and I couldn't find my keys,
I stepped in spilled molasses,
and was stung by angry bees.
When the kitten ripped the curtain,
and the toast burst into flame,
I was absolutely certain
that the clover was to blame.

I buried it discreetly
in the middle of a field,
now my luck has changed completely,
and my wounds have almost healed.
If I ever find another,
I will simply let it be,
or I'll give it to my brother —
he deserves it more than me.

by Jack Prelutsky

What did the character in the poem find out about four-leaf clovers? What were some of the things that happened to him after he found the clover? List the students' responses on the chalkboard.

What does the man decide to do if he ever finds another four-leaf clover? What does that tell you about how he feels about his brother?

Turn to page 78 in your book. Look at the picture of the man. What's happening to him? What does he think is causing all of these "bad luck" things? Look at the picture on page 79. What do you think is under the dirt? Let's read the poem together. Lead the students through several choral readings. Then, for a variation, select students to read individual lines.

Putting Ideas to Work

Things to Talk About

Material
- Page 80 in student book

Look at page 80 in your book. "Things to Talk About" asks us to do some thinking about superstitions.

Read the first set of questions with me. "What did the poet expect to happen after he found the four-leaf clover? What really happened?"

Possible student response — He expected the four-leaf clover to bring him *good* luck, but it really seemed to bring him *bad* luck.

Read the second question with me. "Why does the poet blame the four-leaf clover for his bad luck?"

Possible student response — His bad luck started soon after he found the four-leaf clover.

Read the third question with me. "Who do you blame when unlucky things happen to you?" We all tend to blame someone or something for our bad luck. Who or what do *you* blame?

Some possible student responses — my sister, broken mirrors, myself

Read the fourth question with me. "What advice would you give the poet about superstitions?"

Some possible student responses
a. I'd tell him that since this good-luck sign brought him bad luck, maybe a bad-luck sign will bring him good luck.
b. I'd tell him to ignore them.
c. I'd tell him to try to find another four-leaf clover because the last clover was no good.

Read the fifth set of questions with me. "Do you believe in superstitions? Why? Why not?" Have the students tell if they believe in superstitions and why.

Things to Do *Read choices to classes while they follow along.*

Materials
- Page 80 in student book
- Writing paper
- Pencils
- Drawing paper
- Crayons

Students can choose 2 of these 3 activities to do.

your handout

Look at the "Things to Do" on page 80 in your book. Ask each student to choose one of the three activities to do, or pick one for the whole class to do.

Let's read number 1 together. "Make a list of five things that might have happened to the poet to convince him that four-leaf clovers *do* bring good luck." See if you can think of five good things that might have happened before when the poet had a four-leaf clover. Have the students write lists of good things that happened to the poet when he found a four-leaf clover.

Let's read number 2 together. "Make up two superstitions of your own. One should be about *good luck* and the other should be about *bad luck*. Tell what each superstition is, and draw a picture to go with it." Most superstitions sound crazy to people who don't believe in them, so don't be afraid to be creative with yours! Have the students describe and illustrate their own superstitions.

Fold paper in half

do first 2 together

Good luck   Bad Luck

make guide lines for writing

Let's read number 3 together. "Imagine that the poet finds another four-leaf clover, and he gives it to his brother. What do you think happens to his brother after he receives the clover? Write about it." Have the students write about what happens when the poet gives his brother a four-leaf clover.

Collect work + student copies of poems

Extending Language and Thinking

Activity 1

Objectives
- to identify *good-luck* and *bad-luck* superstitions
- to write creative stories about superstitions

Materials
- Chalkboard and chalk
- Writing paper
- Pencils

On the chalkboard, draw two columns. At the top of one column, write *Good Luck,* and at the top of the other, write *Bad Luck*. Have the students suggest superstitions to list under each column.

Ask each student to choose one of the superstitions on the chalkboard to write about. Have them write ironic pieces, in either poetry or prose form, in which the superstitious event causes the opposite effect than expected. Ask the students to include at least five things that happen that are the opposite of what would be expected.

Activity 2

Objective
- to participate in a group choral reading

Materials
- Pages 78-79 in student book

Clever idea!

Have the students present the poem to another class. Suggest that they change *I, my,* and *me* in stanzas one and four to *we, our,* and *us*. Have the entire class read those stanzas aloud. Assign individual students one or two lines each from the second and third stanzas to read aloud.

Strengthening Language for Second-Language Learners

Activity

Objectives
- to illustrate the events of the poem
- to sequence the events

Materials
- Drawing paper
- Crayons

Discuss the events that take place in stanzas two and three. Then, have individual students illustrate each event. Use these illustrations as visuals for a group reading and a sequencing activity.

Reaching Across the Curriculum

Developing Creative Expression

Activity

Objectives
- to make a survey of familiar superstitions
- to illustrate superstitions

Materials
- Writing paper
- Pencils
- Drawing paper
- Crayons

Encourage each student to survey friends and family for familiar superstitions. Have the students write down the superstitions and illustrate them.

Expanding Social Studies

Activity 1

Objective
- to research types of folklore

Materials
- Library sources

Explain that superstitions are a kind of folklore. No one's quite sure who first thought them up, but they've been around for hundreds of years. Encourage the students to research other types of folklore such as tales about medicinal remedies, weather lore, and folktales. Provide opportunities for the students to share their findings.

Activity 2 *Good one!*

Objective
- to discuss fact versus fantasy in superstitions

Material
- None

The topic of superstition lends itself to a discussion about *fact* and *fantasy*. Analyze the superstitions you have discussed in class. **Could we prove whether or not these superstitions really *do* cause good or bad luck? Why do people believe in superstitions if they can't be proved?**

Expanding Literature

Activity

Objectives
- to share a children's book
- to write a creative story

Materials
- Children's book
  Viorst, Judith. *Alexander and the Terrible, Horrible, No Good, Very Bad Day.*
  New York: Atheneum Publishers, 1976.
- Writing paper
- Pencils

Read Judith Viorst's story with the students. Ask them to compare Alexander's day with the character in "I Found a Four-Leaf Clover."

Use this theme as a springboard for a writing assignment in which the students describe their own "terrible, horrible, no good, very bad" days.

Lesson 28

Foolish Questions

Will your students be able to figure out the humor in the strange questions asked by the poet of this tongue in cheek poem? "Foolish Questions" is a folk rhyme that provides a basis for exploring the multiple meanings of words and for reinforcing the importance of using context to identify word meaning.

Objectives:

Students will
- expand vocabulary by identifying multiple meanings of words.
- practice using context clues.
- practice choral/oral reading.
- differentiate between sense and nonsense.
- strengthen dictionary skills.
- extend language and ideas through oral and written expression.

Warming Up for Reading

Materials
- Large piece of paper
- Bulletin board
- Marker
- Index cards
- Crayons
- Chalkboard and chalk

Post a large piece of paper on a bulletin board. Write *cap* in the middle of the paper. Distribute index cards to the students.

Point to the word *cap*. **I've written the word *cap* on this piece of paper. That should be a familiar word for all of you. On your index card, draw a picture of the first thing that comes to mind when you see or hear the word *cap*.**

Provide adequate time for the students to complete their illustrations. Then, have the students post their drawings around the word *cap*. Have each student describe what she has depicted in her drawing.

If none of the students has drawn a picture of a *kneecap,* tell the students that there is another type of *cap*. Point to your *kneecap*. Ask a volunteer to draw a picture of a *kneecap* to add to the *cap* display. Explain that the word *cap* is an example of the many words in our language that have more than one meaning.

On the chalkboard, write the following sentences.

I collect bottle caps.
I collect baseball caps.
I collect kneecaps.

Which sentences make sense? Which one doesn't? Why? Notice that the word *kneecaps* is one word made up of two smaller words. What do we call this kind of word? What are the two words that make up the compound word *kneecaps?*

Today's poet asks a lot of odd questions about words that have more than one meaning. See if you can figure out which words confuse him.

Sharing the Poem

Materials
- Page 81 in student book
- Chalkboard and chalk

Read the poem in a quizzical voice.

(Turn the page for the poem.)

Foolish Questions

Where can a man buy a cap for his knee?
Or a key for the lock of his hair?
And can his eyes be called a school?
I would think — there are pupils there!
What jewels are found in the crown of his head,
And who walks on the bridge of his nose?
Can he use, in building the roof of his mouth,
The nails on the ends of his toes?
Can the crook of his elbow be sent to jail —
If it can, well, then, what did it do?
And how does he sharpen his shoulder blades?
I'll be hanged if I know — do you?
Can he sit in the shade of the palm of his hand,
And beat time with the drum of his ear?
Can the calf of his leg eat the corn on his toe? —
    There's somethin' pretty strange around here!

An American folk rhyme
adapted by William Cole

Now, you can understand why I said the poet was confused! What are some of the words that confused the poet? List the students' responses on the chalkboard under the title *Word*. The following is an example.

Word
cap   part of knee
      something to wear
      something on a bottle top

Ask the students to find the meaning of each confusing word in the poem and to think of other meanings for that word. On the chalkboard next to each word, write the meaning the word has in the poem and then other meanings for the word.

We'll come back to this chart after we read through the poem. Turn to page 81 in your book. Look at the picture. Why is the person dressed like a king with a crown on his head? Why is he holding a key? Let's read "Foolish Questions" together. Guide the students through the poem. Then, using the poem, have the students locate any multiple-meaning words that they haven't discussed yet. Add these words to the list on the chalkboard. Discuss the meaning each word has in the poem and other meanings for the word. List the meanings on the chalkboard.

Now, let's answer the poet's questions! We'll read the poem aloud again, and after each question we'll stop so that someone can answer it. For example, we'll read, "Where can a man buy a cap for his knee?" Then, one of you might answer, "He can't because a kneecap is part of a body!" Select students to respond to each question. Have them use the information on the chalkboard to help them formulate their answers.

Putting Ideas to Work
Things to Talk About

Material
- Page 82 in student book

Look at page 82 in your book. "Things to Talk About" asks us to do some thinking about the questions the poet asks.

Read number 1 with me. "This poet seems to have a problem. What is it?"

Possible student response — He uses words incorrectly in sentences.

Read number 2 with me. "Which question in the poem is the most ridiculous? Why?"

Some possible student responses
a. "Where can a man buy a cap for his knee?"
   He can't buy a kneecap.
b. "What jewels are found in the crown of his head?"
   The *crown* of his head is the top of his head, not a thing he wears on his head.
c. "And who walks on the bridge of his nose?"
   No one can walk on the top of someone's nose.

Read number 3 with me. "What would you do to help the poet answer his questions?"

Some possible student responses
a. I'd get a dictionary to show him the definitions of the confusing words.
b. I'd act out some of the things the poet says to show him that they don't make sense.
c. I'd explain that the words he's confused about have many meanings.

Things to Do

Materials
- Page 82 in student book
- Drawing paper
- Crayons
- Dictionaries
- Writing paper
- Pencils
- Index cards

Look at the "Things to Do" on page 82 in your book. Ask each student to choose one of the three activities to do, or pick one for the whole class to do.

Let's read number 1 together. "Draw a picture to go with one of the questions asked in the poem." Have the students illustrate the questions from the poem.

Let's read number 2 together. "Write a single sentence using the word lock to show at least *two* of its meanings. Then, try writing a single sentence using the word nail to show at least *three* of its meanings." Provide the students with dictionaries and have them look up the different definitions of *lock* and *nail*. Then, have them write sentences containing these words.

Let's read number 3 together. "Look through the dictionary and find three words that have several meanings each. Write down the different meanings. Then, write each word on a card and show the words to your class. See how many meanings your classmates know. Share the meanings you have found." Have the students find and write down multiple-meaning words and their definitions. Discuss the words and their meanings.

Extending Language and Thinking

Activity

Objective
- to increase understanding of multiple-meaning words

Materials
- Chalkboard and chalk
- Writing paper
- Pencils

On the chalkboard, write *I like to collect pictures of rock groups.*

If you were to read this sentence quickly, what would you think I meant by *rock groups?* Tell me what you think the pictures I collect are like. Accept the students' responses.

I want to tell you a little more about myself. My dad is a geologist. That's a scientist who studies information about the earth's formation. We go camping a lot. We usually take lots of pictures of the earth's surface.

What if I had told you about myself before you read the sentence? Would that change your interpretation of the sentence on the chalkboard? Why?

On the chalkboard, draw the following diagram.

Context is very important in helping us understand the meaning of a word. For instance, the word *block* has several meanings, but only one meaning will make sense in a particular sentence. What are some different definitions of the word *block?* Write the students' responses on the spokes on the chalkboard. Then, have the students work in pairs to compose two sentences, each using a different meaning for *block*. Once they have finished writing, have the students take turns reading their sentences aloud.

Strengthening Language for Second-Language Learners

Activity

Objectives
- to identify multiple meanings of words
- to illustrate multiple meanings

Materials
- Chalkboard and chalk
- Drawing paper
- Crayons

Ask the students to identify instances when they have been confused by hearing or reading multiple-meaning words. List the words they identify on the chalkboard.

On the chalkboard in a separate list, write the words *bank, cut, lap, run, bat,* and *show.* Carefully pronounce each word. Have each student choose one word to illustrate its various meanings. Make sure that all the words are covered. Encourage the students to make up a sentence to correspond with each illustration. Once the students have finished, have them share their illustrations and sentences with the rest of the class.

Reaching Across the Curriculum
Developing Creative Expression

Activity

Objective
- to practice using multiple-meaning words

Materials
- Chalkboard and chalk
- Writing paper
- Pencils
- Dictionaries

On the chalkboard, write the words *bank, run, bat, beat, back,* and *lap*. Have the students write one sentence for each word. Tell them to use each word twice in a sentence to illustrate two different meanings of the word. If necessary, allow the students to use dictionaries. As an example of a sentence using *bank,* a student might write the following. *While I sat on the bank fishing, Fred went to the bank to cash my check.*

Exploring Science

Activity

Objective
- to identify body parts mentioned in the poem

Materials
- Large pieces of paper
- Markers

This activity expands on the information about body parts given in the poem. Begin by dividing the class into groups. Ask for a volunteer in each group to have his body traced onto a large piece of paper. Have each group label the body parts with phrases from the poem such as "lock of his hair" and "crown of his head."

Expanding Literature

Activity

Objectives
- to share a children's book
- to discuss ways to clarify word meaning

Material
- Children's book
  Longman, Harold. *Would you put your money in a sandbank?* Skokie, IL: Rand McNally and Company, 1968.

Would you put your money in a sandbank? is a humorous book to share with your class. Your students should be able to identify with the misunderstandings caused by multiple-meaning words and homonyms. It can also serve as a springboard for the following discussion.

When you're listening to someone speak, what can you do if you're confused by what she's saying? When you're speaking to someone, what do you look for in order to make sure that the person who's listening understands you? What can you do to further clarify what you're saying?

Building Dictionary Skills

Activity

Objective
- to use a dictionary to locate multiple meanings of words

Materials
- A different dictionary for each group
- Writing paper
- Pencils

Divide the class into groups and have them look up the definitions for the same multiple-meaning word. Have the students share their findings. See which group discovers the most definitions of the word.

Lesson 29

Creature Features

Watch your students' eyes come alive as they share the excitement of these *horrific* plots for scary movies.

Objectives:

Students will
- make and verify predictions.
- practice choral/oral reading.
- compare and contrast scary movies.
- extend language and ideas through oral and written expression.

Warming Up for Reading

Materials
- Chalkboard and chalk

On the chalkboard, write *Creature Features*.

Have you ever seen a really scary movie? What is the name of the most frightening *creature feature* you've ever seen or heard about? List the students' responses on the chalkboard.

Why do you think people like to see scary movies? How do you think the writers think up the plots for these *creature features*?

Get ready for some chills and thrills! Today's poem is called "Creature Features." For now, I'm going to read only part of the poem. See if you can figure out who the word "they" refers to in the poem.

Sharing the Poem

Materials
- Pages 83-85 in student book
- Chalkboard and chalk

Read only the chorus to the students.

Read together or rows take parts

Creature Features

They go to horror movies
  And to other scary shows
Because they love each shudder
  From their fingertips to toes.
And when they get together
  And have nothing else to do,
They make up horror movies
  That would scare the hair off you!

They told about a movie
  At the pool inside the gym,
With a monster lying waiting
  For a child to take a swim.
It would open its enormous mouth
  And suck the swimmer in,
Then lay there, give a burp or two,
  And smile a deadly grin.

They go to horror movies
  And to other scary shows
Because they love each shudder
  From their fingertips to toes.
And when they get together
  And have nothing else to do,
They make up horror movies
  That would scare the hair off you!

They told about a movie
  That is not yet on the screen.
There's this very scary monster
  Inside a drink machine.
And when you put your money in,
  Before you even scream,
Twelve tentacles reach out and grab
  And squeeze you till you're green!

They go to horror movies
    And to other scary shows
Because they love each shudder
    From their fingertips to toes.
And when they get together
    And have nothing else to do,
They make up horror movies
    That would scare the hair off you!

They told about a movie
    That has aliens from space.
They had the creatures landing
    And invading Pizza Place.
When you order at the counter,
    They leap up and claw your face;
Your blood's so frozen you can't
    Even get your feet to race!

They go to horror movies
    And to other scary shows
Because they love each shudder
    From their fingertips to toes.
And when they get together
    And have nothing else to do,
They make up horror movies
    That would scare the hair off you!

by Barbara Schmidt

Do you have some idea of who the word "they" refers to in the poem? Help the students understand that the word "they" might refer to children their own age.

The part of the poem that I read talks about making up "horror movies that would scare the hair off you." When I read the rest of the poem you'll hear about some of those movies. Before I begin, tell me what you think will be going on in some of these movies. Write some of the students' ideas on the chalkboard.

Let's see if you came close! Read the entire poem, encouraging the students to provide squeals, screams, and other appropriate sound effects.

Your sound effects certainly added to the scariness! Did you guess what any of the plots to these movies would be? Have the students compare their predictions with the three plots in the poem.

Which of the three plots in the poem do you think would make the best movie? Which was the scariest? Which painted the most vivid picture?

You'll have a chance to make up your own horror movie plots later. Now, it's time to read the poem together. Turn to page 83 in your book. Look at the picture. Which movie is this monster from? Turn to page 84. Where does the monster in this picture live? How do the girls on page 85 feel about what they've seen? Let's read through the poem together. Read the poem in unison adding sound effects. For subsequent readings, have individual students or small groups read stanzas with the whole class chiming in on the chorus. You may also choose to have the students pantomime some of the movie plots.

Putting Ideas to Work

Things to Talk About

Material
- Page 86 in student book

Look at page 86 in your book. "Things to Talk About" asks us to do some thinking about scary movies.

Read the first set of questions with me. "Which of the three movie ideas was your favorite? Why?"

Some possible student responses
a. The first one is my favorite because it's really scary.
b. The second one is my favorite because it's different from any other scary movie I've seen or heard about.
c. The third one is my favorite because I like movies about aliens.

Read the second set of questions with me. "Would you read this poem to a younger brother or sister? Why? Why not?"

Some possible student responses
a. Yes, I like to scare my little brother.
b. No, the poem is too scary for younger children.

Read the third set of questions with me. "What are some good things about scary movies? What are some things that are not so good?" First, tell some good things about scary movies.

Some possible student responses
a. Scary movies are usually full of adventure.
b. Scary movies make you use your imagination.

Now, what are some "not-so-good" things about scary movies?

Some possible student responses
a. They make some people have bad dreams.
b. Some people might believe that these scary things can really happen.

Read the fourth set of questions with me. "How do your parents feel about scary movies? Why do they feel that way?"

Some possible student responses
a. My parents like scary movies, but they don't let me watch them because they think I'll have bad dreams.
b. My parents like scary movies because they like *all* kinds of movies.
c. My parents don't like scary movies because they think they're stupid.

Things to Do

Materials
- Page 86 in student book
- Writing paper
- Pencils
- Poster board
- Markers

Look at the "Things to Do" on page 86 in your book. Ask each student to choose one of the three activities to do, or pick one for the whole class to do.

 Let's read number 1 together. "Pick your favorite movie idea from the poem. Imagine that you are writing a screenplay for this movie. Make a title for your movie. Write a description of what happens in the movie." Have the students write descriptions of the movie ideas from the poem.

 Let's read number 2 together. "Make a poster advertising one of the movie ideas in the poem." You'll need to make up a title for the movie, and just for fun, you might want to list some famous actors who are starring in the movie. Have the students make posters advertising the movies.

Let's read number 3 together. "Make a list of the scariest movies you have ever seen. Compare your list with a friend's. Did you and your friend list any movies that are the same? What do the movies you chose have in common with your friend's? What's different about the movies you chose from the ones your friend chose?" Have the students write lists of scary movies. Then, have them compare and discuss their lists with partners.

Extending Language and Thinking

Activity

Objectives
- to create vivid monster descriptions
- to invent ways to get rid of monsters

Materials
- Chalkboard and chalk
- Writing paper
- Pencils
- Drawing paper
- Crayons

On the chalkboard, write the following.

Part 1 — Create a monster!
Part 2 — Get rid of the monster!

We're going to play a monster game. There are two parts to the game. Read the parts listed on the chalkboard. Explain to the students that for the first part of the game, each team should think up five *very* vivid descriptions of imaginary monsters. Pick one member of the team to write down each description. Tell the students not to write just *big* or *ugly*. Tell them to write something like *a fire-breathing creature with a scaly body.* Have them leave several lines between each description. Give the students time to write their descriptions, and then continue the activity.

Now, it's time to "Get rid of the monster!" Have each team pass their descriptions to another team. That team must think up a way to get rid of each monster described.

Have one person from each team write down how to get rid of each monster underneath the description. If the other team's description is a *hideous beast with three-foot-long claws,* the team scribe might write *Give it a manicure!*

When the students have completed this activity, discuss their monster descriptions and ways of getting rid of the monsters.

As an extension of this activity, have the students illustrate their monsters and write stories about them.

Strengthening Language for Second-Language Learners

Activity

Objective
- to develop understanding of parts of speech and sentence structure

Materials
- Chalkboard and chalk

On the chalkboard, write the following.

_____   _____
_____ *monsters* _____
_____   _____

Point to the lines on the left side of the chalkboard. **I need help filling in these blanks. Close your eyes and try to picture a terrible monster. Now, open your eyes and tell me what the monster looked like. Use vividly descriptive adjectives.** On the left side of the chalkboard, write the adjectives supplied by the students. Then, ask the students to chant their descriptions. Point to each adjective and then to the word *monster.* (For example, the students might say **scary monsters, hairy monsters, green monsters,** etc.)

Now, we need to fill in the blanks on the right side of the chalkboard. This time give me words that tell what monsters *do*. Use action verbs or verb phrases. On the chalkboard, write the verbs or verb phrases. Tell the students to say the words you point to on the chalkboard. Then, point to an adjective, the word *monster,* and a verb or verb phrase. Explain that combining these words forms a sentence.

This is a valuable activity for developing an understanding of parts of speech and sentence structure. Ask the students to make up sentences using combinations of words from the chalkboard.

Reaching Across the Curriculum

Developing Creative Expression

Activity 1

Objective
- to write and dramatize a mini monster movie

Materials
- Writing paper
- Pencils
- Simple props

Have the students write a mini monster movie, which they will dramatize using props, costumes, and scenery. If possible, videotape the production so that the students can see their own performances and so that other classes might be able to enjoy the production whenever they want.

Activity 2

Objective
- to dramatically retell monster stor___

Material
- Tape recorder

Using a tape recorder, have the students retell the plots of favorite monster movies for scary listening. Encourage the students to use expressively dramatic voices in their recitations.

Activity 3

Objective
- to use words to describe feelings

Materials
- Writing paper
- Pencils
- Chalkboard and chalk

Have the students write lists of words that describe feelings they've experienced while watching scary movies. List these words on the chalkboard. Compare the words and decide which words paint the most vivid pictures in a person's mind.

Expanding Social Studies

Activity

Objective
- to distinguish reality from fantasy in facts and fiction

Materials
- Library sources
- Writing paper
- Pencils

This selection offers a good opportunity to distinguish *reality* from *fantasy*. Have the students research topics relating to beliefs people hold about the existence of monsters such as the Loch Ness Monster, Bigfoot, Dracula, and Frankenstein. Have the students share the information they find. Discuss and evaluate its validity.

Expanding Literature and Art

Activity

Objectives
- to share monster tales
- to create visuals for the monster tales

Materials
- Monster books
- Art supplies

Share a folktale, fairy tale, or myth about a monster. Explain that tales about monsters have been around for years. Have the students locate monster stories in the library and read them. Have each student choose one story to tell the class. Have the students create visuals such as masks, costumes, or hats to enhance their presentations.

Lesson 30

The Wise Men and the Elephant

Your students will discover that things are not always as they seem in this encounter with "The Wise Men and the Elephant." This humorous classic has a serious message about drawing conclusions before you have all the facts.

Objectives:

Students will

- use the sense of touch to identify objects.
- extend vocabulary.
- practice choral/oral reading.
- recall details from the poem.
- create descriptive paragraphs.
- extend language and ideas through oral and written expression.

Warming Up for Reading

Materials
- Paper grocery bag containing various objects
- Blindfold

Put the grocery bag where the students can see it.

I need your help for an experiment I call "What is it?" Here's how it works. I'll place a blindfold over someone's eyes. When I'm sure that this person can't see what I'm doing, I'll take an object out of this bag. Then, I'll have the person feel the object by using only one finger to touch the surface. The person should tell us if the object feels rough or smooth, warm or cold, etc. After that, the person can guess what the object is. After she guesses, I'll remove her blindfold and let her choose someone else to continue the experiment. Are you ready to try it out?

Select a student to begin the activity. Take an object out of the grocery bag, and hold it out for the blindfolded student to touch. Do not let the student use more than one finger to feel the object. Have her guess what the object is. Continue the activity with several students.

Were some of the objects difficult to identify by using only one finger to feel them? What couldn't you learn about some of the objects by just touching them? If necessary, explain that the feel of something doesn't tell you what color(s) it is, how much it weighs, etc.

Our experiment reminds me of the expression "Never judge a book by its cover." What does this expression mean to you?

What does this experiment tell us about making judgments and drawing conclusions about things when we don't have all the facts? Make sure that the students understand that the lesson to be learned by this experiment is that first impressions are not always correct.

There is a poem in our book about six unusual men who have a new experience when they meet and touch an elephant for the very first time. Close your eyes as I read the poem. Listen carefully to how each man describes the elephant.

Sharing the Poem

Materials
- Pages 87-88 in student book
- Chalkboard and chalk

After instructing the students to close their eyes and listen carefully, read the selection aloud to them.

The Wise Men and the Elephant

It was six men of Hindustan,
To learning much inclined,
Who went to see the elephant,
(Though all of them were blind),
That each by observation
Might satisfy the mind.

The first approached the elephant,
And, happening to fall
Against its broad and sturdy side,
At once began to bawl:
"Why, bless me! but the elephant
Is very like a wall!"

The second, feeling at the tusk,
Cried, "Ho! what have we here
So very round and smooth and sharp?
To me 'tis mighty clear
This wonder of an elephant
Is very like a spear!"

The third approached the animal,
And, happening to take
The squirming trunk within his hands,
Thus boldly up he spake:
"I see," quoth he, "the elephant
Is very like a snake!"

The fourth reached out his eager hand,
And felt about its knee.
"What most this wondrous beast is like
Is mighty plain," quoth he:
" 'Tis clear enough the elephant
Is very like a tree!"

The fifth, who chanced to touch the ear,
Said: "E'en the blindest man
Can tell what this resembles most;
Deny the fact who can,
This marvel of an elephant
Is very like a fan!"

The sixth no sooner had begun
About the beast to grope,
Than, seizing on the swinging tail
That fell within his scope,
"I see," quoth he, "the elephant
Is very like a rope!"

And so these men of Hindustan
Disputed loud and long,
Each in his own opinion
Exceeding stiff and strong;
Though each was partly in the right,
They all were in the wrong!

by John G. Saxe

How were the six men alike? Did they all agree that what they were touching was an elephant? Why not?

Let's read about their strange experience. Turn to page 87 in your book. Look at the picture. What part of the elephant is the man touching? What does he think it feels like? Turn to page 88. What part of the elephant is this man touching? What does he think it feels like? Join me in reading the poem aloud. Read the poem aloud with the students.

On the chalkboard, write the following words and phrases from the poem.

to learning much inclined
'tis
spake
e'en

There are some strange words and expressions in this poem. I've written some of them on the chalkboard. For example, the poem says that the men were *"to learning much inclined."* What do you think this expression means? Explain that this phrase means *eager to learn.*

I've also written *'tis* on the chalkboard. In the third stanza, one of the wise men says "to me *'tis* mighty clear." *'Tis* is a contraction. Do you know what two words make up the contraction? If necessary, explain that *'tis* is a combination of the words *it* and *is.*

In the fourth stanza, the poet uses the word *spake*. What does that mean? Why didn't he use the word *spoke* instead of *spake*? Help the students understand that the poet used *spake* because it rhymes with *take* and *snake.*

In the sixth stanza, one of the men says, "*E'en* the blindest man can tell what this resembles most." What do you thing *e'en* means? Why didn't the poet use the word *even* instead of *e'en*? Point out that the second, fourth, and sixth lines of each stanza contain six beats per line. Using *even* instead of *e'en* would add an extra beat to this line and throw off the rhythm of the poem.

Let's divide the poem into reading parts and practice reading it aloud. I'll need six "wise" students to read what each man says. How do you know when a character in the poem is speaking? Point out that speaking parts are in quotes. Then, assign the speaking parts to individual students and have the rest of the class read the narrated parts of the poem.

Putting Ideas to Work

Things to Talk About

Materials
- Page 89 in student book
- Chalkboard and chalk

Look at page 89 in your book. "Things to Talk About" asks us to do some thinking about "The Wise Men and the Elephant."

Read the first set of questions with me. "What did each man think the elephant resembled? Why did each man think the elephant was like that?"

Possible student responses
a. The first thought the elephant resembled a wall because its side was "broad and sturdy."
b. The second thought the elephant resembled a spear because its tusk felt "smooth and sharp."
c. The third thought the elephant resembled a snake because its trunk was "squirming."
d. The fourth thought the elephant resembled a tree because he felt the elephant's knee.
e. The fifth thought the elephant resembled a fan because he felt the elephant's ear.
f. The sixth thought the elephant resembled a rope because he felt the elephant's tail.

Read the second question with me. "Which man do you think came up with the most unusual comparison?"

Some possible student responses — the second man, the fourth man, the fifth man

Read the third question with me. "How would you help these men have a better understanding of what an elephant is like?" Remember, these men are blind.

Some possible student responses
a. I would describe what an elephant looks like.
b. I would tell them to feel the *whole* elephant, not just part of it.
c. I would tell them where each of the things they felt is on the elephant's body.

Read the fourth question with me. "How would *you* describe an elephant to someone who had never seen one before?" Each of you should tell me one fact about elephants. I'll write each fact on the chalkboard. When we're through, we'll have a lot of information about elephants!

Some possible student responses
a. African elephants are the largest animals that live on land.
b. Elephants are huge gray animals with trunks.
c. Elephants have wrinkly skin and are very heavy.

Things to Do ✏

Materials

- Page 89 in student book
- Writing paper
- Pencils
- Books about blind people

Look at the "Things to Do" on page 89 in your book. Ask each student to choose one of the four activities to do, or pick one for the whole class to do.

Let's read number 1 together. "Write five different endings to the following sentence. *The elephant is like _____ ."* The men in the poem completed this sentence with pretty strange comparisons. One compared an elephant to a wall, and another compared it to a rope. The words you choose to complete your sentences can sound silly, like the ones in the poem. As long as you can explain your choices, it's okay. Have each student complete the sentence in five different ways.

Let's read number 2 together. "Write a short paragraph describing what your life would be like if you couldn't see. What are some things you do now that you wouldn't be able to do? What are some things you would still be able to do?" Have the students write paragraphs about how their lives would be different if they were blind.

Let's read number 3 together. "Read a story or biography about a blind person. Find out what this person was able to accomplish despite his or her handicap." Have the students read about blind people.

Let's read number 4 together. "Write a short story about a blind person who uses his or her sense of touch to describe one of the following animals: a. a giraffe, b. a crocodile, c. a hippopotamus, d. an ostrich." Have the students write short stories about blind people using the sense of touch to describe animals.

Extending Language and Thinking

Activity 1

Objective

- to dramatize the poem

Materials

- Picture of the side view of an elephant
- Opaque projector
- Large piece of paper
- Tape
- Pencil
- Crayons
- Pages 87-88 in student book

Locate a picture showing the side view of an elephant. Using an opaque projector, project this picture onto a large sheet of paper taped to the wall. Have a student trace the outline of the elephant onto the paper. Other students can participate by lightly coloring the outline and adding detailed features.

Once this representation has been completed, assign six students to play the roles of the six blind men. Line the six students up next to the picture of the elephant. As the rest of the class reads the poem aloud, have the six "blind men" act out their parts.

As a variation, have the six students playing the parts of the wise men read aloud the words spoken by the men they portray. They may also wish to memorize their lines.

Activity 2

Objective

- to create new versions of the poem

Materials

- Pages 87-88 in student book
- Writing paper
- Pencils
- Drawing paper
- Crayons

Divide the class into groups of eight students each. Each group should discuss how to rewrite the poem by substituting a new animal, new characters, and a new setting. Each student in a group should rewrite one stanza. Point out that the substitution of new words may throw off the poem's original rhyme pattern and beat. Encourage each student to experiment with her own words and ideas to see if she can follow the rhyme pattern and beat of the poem.

Have each group present their new version of the poem to the class. Each group may wish to draw a picture of the animal in their poem to use as a backdrop for their presentation.

Strengthening Language for Second-Language Learners

Activity 1

Objectives
- to promote sight-word recognition
- to foster understanding of word meaning

Materials
- Chalkboard and chalk

We're going to play a game called "Smaller than an Elephant." What things can you think of that are smaller than an elephant? List the students' responses on the chalkboard.

On the chalkboard, write the following sentence frame.

A _____ is smaller than an elephant.

Tell the students to fill in the blank in the sentence with each word you point to on the chalkboard. Have the students read the entire sentence each time.

Then, erase the word *smaller* in the sentence and replace it with the word *larger*. The sentence should now look like the following.

A _____ is larger than an elephant.

Now, we're going to play a game called "Larger than an Elephant." What things can you think of that are larger than an elephant? They can be names of things rather than animals. List the students' responses on the chalkboard. Tell the students to fill in the blank in the sentence with each word you point to on the chalkboard. Have the students read the entire sentence each time.

Write the following sentence frame on the chalkboard.

A _____ is smaller than an elephant but larger than a _____ .

Have the students use the words listed on the chalkboard to fill in the blanks in the sentence. Have the students read the entire sentence each time they fill in words.

Activity 2

Objective
- to write sentences describing the elephant

Materials
- Chalkboard and chalk
- Writing paper
- Pencils

Have the students brainstorm a list of words that describe what an elephant looks like and how it acts. Record their responses on the chalkboard. Then, have the students construct sentences about the elephant using the words and phrases written on the chalkboard.

Reaching Across the Curriculum

Developing Creative Expression

Activity

Objective
- to write imaginative stories about the elephant's trunk

Materials
- Writing paper
- Pencils

Have the students write short imaginative stories about how the elephant got its trunk. Tell the students to explain how the elephant got such a long trunk.

Have the students use the following steps.

1. Write a rough draft.
2. Read the rough draft to see if it makes sense and to correct spelling and punctuation.
3. Share the rough draft with someone to see if she has some suggestions for improvement.

4. Rewrite any parts that are unclear.
5. Write a final draft.
6. Present the story to the class.

Exploring Science

Activity

Objective
- to utilize the five senses

Materials
- Chalkboard and chalk
- Onion
- Paper bag
- Common object
- Sugar and salt
- Two small bowls

Have the students identify the five senses *(hearing, sight, smell, touch, taste)*. Write them on the chalkboard.

Discuss what life would be like without the sense of sight. Stress the fact that blind people compensate for the lack of sight by relying on their other senses. The following exercises illustrate this point.

Have the students shut their eyes. Tell them that you are going to walk to various spots in the room. When you stop, say **Where am I?** Tell the students to point to you without opening their eyes. After walking to various spots and having the students locate your positions, discuss how they knew where you were even though they couldn't see you. Have them determine the sense they used.

Cut up an onion and place it in the paper bag. Have the students close their eyes and pass the bag around the room. No one should be allowed to talk during this time. After everyone has had a chance to hold the bag, ask the students to identify its contents. Discuss how they knew it was an onion even though they couldn't see it. Have them determine the sense they used.

Place a common object in the paper bag. Have the students close their eyes and pass the bag around the room. Tell the students not to talk during this time. Have the students try to identify what is in the bag. After everyone has

had a chance to hold the bag, ask the students what they think is in the bag. Have them determine the sense they used.

Place some sugar and salt in two separate bowls. Explain that these substances are things they can eat. Ask the students to find out what the substances are. Have them determine the sense they used.

Expanding Social Studies

Objective
- to promote understanding of handicaps

Material
- Resource person

Invite a resource person to visit the class to discuss how blind people or deaf people learn to function in society. This visitation could provide an introduction to a unit on Understanding Handicaps. Other handicaps people have and how they adapt to them could be discussed.

Expanding Literature

Activity

Objective
- to identify characteristics of story-poems

Materials
- Library books

This selection is a good example of a "story-poem." Have the students locate and share other story-poems and ballads with the class. The following are some suggested selections:

"The Charge of the Light Brigade"
  (Alfred, Lord Tennyson)
"Casey at the Bat" (Ernest L. Thayer)
"Paul Revere's Ride" (Henry Wadsworth
  Longfellow)
"The Highwayman" (Alfred Noyes)
"Tom Dooley" (folk ballad)
"Sixteen Tons" (folk ballad)
"Aunt Rhody" (folk ballad)

Lesson 31

The Test

This poem about a student's anxiety over a vocabulary test may cause *your* students to break out in a cold sweat as they identify with this traumatic experience. "The Test" provides an opportunity for students to discuss their own feelings about taking tests.

Objectives:

Students will
- identify the emotions of the boy in the poem.
- practice choral/oral reading.
- identify test-taking strategies.
- make predictions based on information in the poem.
- extend language and ideas through oral and written expression.

Warming Up for Reading

Materials
- Chalkboard and chalk

On the chalkboard, write *camelopard*.

I need everyone's attention now! We're having a surprise test today!

Mrs. Rosendale left us

Point to the word *camelopard*. **This is one of several words that you will be asked to define in today's test. I see some puzzled looks on your faces! You look as if you've never seen this word before. As a matter of fact, I hadn't heard of this word either until I read today's poem. This is how you pronounce it — kə mel′ ə pard. Say it with me.** Guide the students in practicing the pronunciation of *camelopard*.

Sharing the Poem

Materials
- Pages 90-91 in student book

Read the poem expressively.

The Test

**Oh, what a week! Oh, what a week!
I'm so confused. It's hard to speak.**

My English teacher, Ms. Dismay,
Is giving us a test today.

I've studied 'til I'm almost nuts,
And yet I feel like such a klutz!

And now she's handing out the test,
I'm too upset to do my best.

This list is long! The words are hard.
The first word is "ca-mel-o-pard."

Is that another name for a cow?
Or is it something used to plow?

I must stay cool just like Tom.
This English test I mustn't bomb.

My mind's in gear; I clearly see
These words are not a mystery.

"Camelopard" . . . is a giraffe.
A metal hook . . . is called a "gaff."
A "guffaw" is . . . a hearty laugh.
The husks of grain . . . are called the "chaff."

To "domesticate" . . . means to tame.
To "humiliate" . . . is to shame.
While to "criticize" . . . is to blame.
And to "mutilate" . . . means to maim.

**Oh, what a week! Oh, what a week!
I feel so good. It's hard to speak!**

I think I've aced this English test.
I know I've done my very best.

(continued)

What's that you say? What's that you say?
You gave us the wrong test today?

Oh, what a week! Oh, what a week!
I'm so confused. It's hard to speak!

I cannot take another test.
I'm too worn out; I need to rest!

by Maurice Poe

**Why is the student in the poem so *confused?*
What happens? Why does the student go
from feeling confused to feeling good to
feeling confused again?**

Read the old poem. *(handwritten)*

Pass out poem *(handwritten)*

**Turn to page 90 in your book. Look at the
picture of the boy. How does he look? Why
does he look that way? Look at the picture
of the camelopard on page 91. What is a
camelopard?**

**Let's read the poem together. We'll begin
by reading slowly, using our voices to
show how upset we are. Then, as we read
the part that shows the meaning of the
words, we'll read a little faster and use
confident, self-assured voices. When we
come to the part where we think we've
"aced" the test, we'll use excited voices.
Then, we'll slow down again and sound
discouraged at the end of the poem.** Guide
the students through an expressive group
reading.

Ask volunteers to read the poem to the rest of
the class. Each volunteer should come to the
front of the room and present his interpretation.
After each reading, have the students discuss
the quality of the presentation. They should
identify positive points about the presentations
and suggest ways that the presentations could
be improved.

a lot for 1 person! maybe take have 3 people switch turns - switch every stanza (handwritten)

Putting Ideas to Work
Things to Talk About

Material
- Page 92 in student book

**Look at page 92 in your book. "Things to
Talk About" asks us to do some thinking
about tests.**

**Read the first set of questions with me.
"Do you become 'confused' when you take
a test? Why? Why not?"**

Some possible student responses
a. Yes, I often can't remember the answers even
   though I've studied.
b. No, I always study for my tests.
c. Yes, sometimes I don't understand the
   questions.

**Read the second question with me. "What
advice could you give to help this person
relax more when taking a test?"**

Some possible student responses
a. For practice, I'd tell him to have someone
   quiz him before the test.
b. I'd tell him to breathe deeply.
c. I'd tell him to read the questions slowly and
   take time to carefully think about the answers.

**Read the third set of questions with me.
"What do you think caused the teacher to
give the wrong test? What do you think the
teacher did after announcing that the
wrong test had been given?" First, tell us
why you think the teacher gave the wrong
test.**

Some possible student responses
a. He took the wrong test out of his folder of
   tests.
b. A mischievous student switched the test
   when the teacher wasn't looking.
c. He got his test mixed up with another
   teacher's.

Now, tell what you think the teacher did after he realized that he gave the wrong test?

Some possible student responses
a. He threw away the wrong test and handed out the right test.
b. He decided not to grade the test but went over the correct answers with the class.
c. He decided to collect the tests and to use them as extra credit.

Things to Do

Materials
- Page 92 in student book
- Writing paper
- Pencils
- Drawing paper
- Crayons

Look at the "Things to Do" on page 92 in your book. Ask each student to choose one of the three activities to do, or pick one for the whole class to do. _All_

Let's read number 1 together. "Make a list of things you do to prepare for a test. Share your list with the class." Have the students list things they do to prepare for tests. Discuss their ideas.

Let's read number 2 together. "Did you know that more than fifty words can be spelled using the letters in 'camelopard'? How many can you spell? Write them down. Proper nouns and abbreviations are not allowed, but you can use each letter more than once in a word." Have the students write lists of words using the letters in "camelopard."

Let's read number 3 together. "The word 'camelopard' sounds like the name of an animal that is part camel and part leopard. Make up a new animal name by combining the names of two familiar animals. Then, write a description of this new animal. Tell what it looks like, where it is found, some

of its habits, whether it is friendly or dangerous, and why this animal should become your school's mascot. Draw a picture to accompany your description." Have the students write about and draw pictures of imaginary animals.

Extending Language and Thinking

Activity

Objective
- to identify ways to improve vocabulary

Materials
- Chart paper
- Marker
- Bulletin board
- Index cards
- Pencils

This selection provides an opportunity to discuss the importance of improving one's vocabulary. Ask the students to discuss techniques they use to learn and remember words. Write the following helpful steps on a chart.

1. _Try to guess the meaning of the word from the way it's used in a sentence._
2. _Look it up in a dictionary._
3. _Ask someone the meaning of the word._
4. _Learn the meaning of the root word of an unfamiliar word._
5. _Learn the meanings of the most common prefixes._
6. _Use new words immediately. Say them out loud. Write them in your own sentences._

Post this chart on a bulletin board. Have the students write new words they encounter on index cards to be posted on the bulletin board. Tell the students to write a word and its pronunciation on the front of the card. Each word card will then have the word and its phonetic spelling on the front. On the back, have the students write the definition of the word and a sentence containing the word.

Strengthening Language for Second-Language Learners

Activity

Objective
- to discuss nerve-racking situations

Materials
- Chalkboard and chalk

Ask the students to talk about situations that make them nervous and uneasy.

On the chalkboard, write the following sentence frames.

I get nervous when _____ .
I find I am less nervous when _____ .

Have the students complete the sentences orally. (For example, **I get nervous when I give a talk in class. I find I am less nervous when I practice giving my talk at home.**)

Reaching Across the Curriculum

Developing Creative Expression

Activity 1

Objective
- to create new versions of the chorus

Materials
- Chalkboard and chalk

On the chalkboard, write the following sentences from the poem.

Oh, what a week! Oh, what a week!
I'm so confused. It's hard to speak!

Have the students read the lines aloud. Then, have them count the number of beats per line and identify the rhyming words at the end of each line.

On the chalkboard, write the following sentence frames.

Oh, what a _____ ! Oh, what a _____ !
I _____ _____ _____ ! I _____ _____ _____ !

Ask the students to suggest words that might be placed in the blank spaces. Remind them that each line should contain the same number of

beats and that the last word in each of the two lines should rhyme. Read the following examples to the students to help them get started.

Oh, what a day! Oh, what a day!
I feel so sick. I cannot play!

Oh, what a test! Oh, what a test!
I hope I passed. I tried my best!

Activity 2

Objectives
- to foster understanding of word meaning
- to condense information into one sentence

Materials
- Chalkboard and chalk

On the chalkboard, write the following words from the poem.

gaff	*humiliate*
guffaw	*criticize*
chaff	*mutilate*
domesticate	

Discuss the meanings of these words with the students.

On the chalkboard, write the following groups of sentences. Ask the students to read each group of sentences aloud. Then, have them combine each group of sentences into a single sentence.

1. *Do not fold this test.*
   Do not bend this test.
   Do not mutilate this test.

2. *Don't humiliate me.*
   Don't criticize me in front of friends.
   Don't criticize me in front of strangers.

3. *Tom was fishing.*
   Tom used a gaff.
   Tom pulled in a rubber boot.
   Tom guffawed at his catch.

4. *It is hard to domesticate a wolf.*
   A wolf is a wild animal.
   A wolf does not adjust well to being held captive.

Expanding Social Studies

Activity

Objectives
- to examine stress-producing situations
- to identify ways to reduce stress

Materials
- Chalkboard and chalk
- Writing paper
- Pencils

On the chalkboard, write the word *stress*.

Have you ever heard people use this word? What does it mean to you? Accept the students' responses. Emphasize that *stress* is often used to describe feeling pressured, nervous, and/or anxious.

What are some things that make you feel nervous or anxious? List a few of the students' responses on the chalkboard. Then, divide the class into small groups. Have each group brainstorm a list of about eight to ten stress-producing situations. Have them rank the listed items, with *1* the most stress-producing and *10* the least stress-producing.

Lead a class discussion centered around each group's top two stress-producing situations. Have the students suggest ways of reducing stress. A situation and ways to reduce stress might be similar to the following.

Situation — Changing schools

Ways to reduce stress —
a. Get to know new people.
b. Pick out someone in the class and ask him questions about the school.
c. Find out about school activities.

Lesson 32

Space Rockers

Music plays an important role in the lives of students. "Space Rockers" offers an opportunity for the students to discuss individual reactions and tastes as they explore the realm of music together. The "out-of-sight" rock group in this poem will appeal to their interests and imaginations.

Objectives:

Students will
- relate personal experiences.
- extend vocabulary.
- practice choral/oral reading.
- compare and contrast musical interests and tastes.
- extend language and ideas through oral and written expression.

Warming Up for Reading

Materials
- Chalkboard and chalk

Who listens to music on the radio? I knew a lot of hands would go up, including mine! What's your favorite musical group? Did you ever wonder how groups think up their names?

I read a poem that I think you're going to enjoy. It's about some girls who are surprised by a free rock concert. The concert is performed by a group called the "Space Rockers," otherwise known as "Igneous and the Metamorphics."

On the chalkboard, write *Igneous and the Metamorphics.* There's a joke in the group's name. If you know anything about rocks that are found on the ground, you may have heard two words that are used to describe rocks, "igneous" and "metamorphic." When the poet named this band, she was making a joke by using the names of words that describe real rocks to describe a rock group.

As I read the poem, see if you can figure out why "Space Rockers" is a good name for this group.

Sharing the Poem

Materials
- Pages 93-95 in student book

Read the poem aloud to the students.

Space Rockers

You say you've heard some music
   that you thought was out of sight?
I bet it can't compare to what
   we heard the other night.
And if you don't believe me,
   check with Sue or Beth or Gail.
The four of us were camping all alone
   at Deer Springs Trail.
We weren't supposed to be there.
   There was no one else around.
When all at once, our ears picked up
   the most unearthly sound.
A weird and glowing light was pulsing,
   lighting up the sky.
No way that we could sleep that night.
   We didn't even try!

We heard:
Doo-wah-diddie, then, sha-boom, sha-boom,
Whoa-dee-oh-doah, then, va-voom, va-voom.
Shaking and twisting all over the place,
It's the rock-and-roll band from outer space!

Though we were scared, we had to look.
    We crawled on trembling knees.
And when we got up close, we hid
    for cover in the trees.
Sue gasped, Beth choked, and Gail said,
    "This has got to be a dream!"
'Cause right before our eyes we saw
    the most amazing scene.
We saw Igneous, the leader, beating time
    with all his tails.
While his band, the Metamorphics, strummed
    the music on their scales.
The drummer used ten tentacles
    for his percussion sound,
While the Thing who played the guitar
    kind of slithered on the ground.

We heard:
Doo-wah-diddie, then, sha-boom, sha-boom,
Whoa-dee-oh-doah, then, va-voom, va-voom.
Shaking and twisting all over the place,
It's the rock-and-roll band from outer space!

And when a creature grabbed the mike
    and started in to sing,
We knew we'd never heard the likes
    of how that band could swing.
They each wore dark sunglasses and
    a gold jacket with a name.
And the music that they played that night
    was anything but tame.
They rocked and rolled, and we could tell
    that band was really hot.
When we went back next morning,
    they had left a big burned spot.
We couldn't find another thing
    except some shiny stars
With print that said "Space Rockers open
    Friday night on Mars!"

We heard:
Doo-wah-diddie, then, sha-boom, sha-boom,
Whoa-dee-oh-doah, then, va-voom, va-voom.
Shaking and twisting all over the place,
It's the rock-and-roll band from outer space!

by Barbara Schmidt

This group doesn't sound like one that you're likely to see and hear in videos! Where do you think they came from? Where will the band be appearing next?

Let's join the four girls for the concert. Turn to page 93 in your book. Can you remember the names of these girls? Find their names on this page. Turn to page 94. How do the girls look? What made them feel that way? What does one of the girls find on page 95? Find the part of the poem that tells about the two strange events that startled the campers. What does "unearthly" mean? Where might an "unearthly sound" come from? What does it mean when it says the "light was pulsing"?

Find the part of the poem that tells about the drummer. He used "ten tentacles for his percussion sound." What are "tentacles" and what is "percussion sound"?

Let's read the poem together. Then, we'll ask for volunteers to pantomime the actions of the girls and the members of the band. Read the poem in unison. Select individual students to pantomime the actions of the girls and the band members as the rest of the class reads the poem aloud.

Putting Ideas to Work

Things to Talk About

Material
● Page 96 in student book

Look at page 96 in your book. "Things to Talk About" asks us to do some thinking about the "Space Rockers."

Read number 1 with me. "Imagine that you are the agent for 'Igneous' and 'the Metamorphics,' and you are trying to convince a club owner to hire your band. Describe the band to the owner." Remember, you want to tell why your band is special enough to draw people to the club! What are some things you would tell the club owner about Igneous and the Metamorphics?

Some possible student responses
a. "This is the wildest band in the universe!"
b. "This band is so hot that it burns holes in the ground!"
c. "You won't believe the awesome sound the drummer can make with ten tentacles!"

Read number 2 with me. "How do the 'Space Rockers' remind you of other musical groups you've seen or heard?"

Some possible student responses
a. They play rock music.
b. They wear cool outfits.
c. They have a wild light show.

Read number 3 with me. "How does the name 'Space Rockers' fit this musical group?"

Possible student response — This rock group's from outer space.

Read number 4 with me. "Do you think that anyone will believe the girls when they describe their adventure?"

Possible student response — no

Things to Do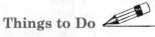

Materials
- Page 96 in student book
- Writing paper
- Pencils
- Poster board
- Markers

Look at the "Things to Do" on page 96 in your book. Ask each student to choose one of the four activities to do, or pick one for the whole class to do.

Let's read number 1 together. "Make up your own chorus for this poem. Try to write some phrases that use words for musical sounds. Use your chorus for a reading of the poem." Look at the chorus of the poem. Do you see how the poet used words for musical sounds, like "doo-wah-diddie" and "sha-boom, sha-boom"? Try to think of some other silly musical sounds to

use in a new version of the chorus. Have the students write new versions of the chorus to use in future readings of the poem.

Let's read number 2 together. "Work with a partner to create a list of your favorite musical groups. Compare your list with another team's. Decide which groups are your all-time favorites." Have the students list and compare their favorite musical groups.

Let's read number 3 together. "Describe the singer for the 'Space Rockers.' What does *it* look like? What songs does *it* sing?" Have the students write about the singer for the Space Rockers.

Let's read number 4 together. "Make a poster advertising the Space Rockers' next concert on Mars." Have the students make posters.

Extending Language and Thinking

Activity 1

Objective
- to conduct musical research

Materials
- Chalkboard and chalk
- Library sources and other resources
- Writing paper
- Pencils

On the chalkboard, write the following column headings.

Kind of Music	Name of Performer or Band	Radio Stations	Description of Music

Let's write something under each heading using information from the poem. What goes under the first column? How about the second column? Write this information on the chalkboard.

Since we haven't heard Igneous and the Metamorphics on any local radio stations, we don't have anything to write in the third column. What about the fourth column? What are some words that describe rock-and-roll? Write the students' responses in the fourth column.

Rock-and-roll is only one type of music. What are some other types?

You're going to conduct your own musical research. Copy the columns I've begun on the chalkboard onto your paper. Try to find out information about as many different kinds of music as you can. For each kind of music, fill in the columns with names of performers, radio stations that might play that kind of music, and words that describe the music. Where could you find information like this? Point out that this information could be gathered by listening to the radio, talking to friends and family, using library sources, etc. Give the students time to locate information. Then, at a specified time, discuss the information that the students have gathered.

Activity 2

Objective
- to research a particular musical group

Materials
- Magazine and newspaper articles

If you had ten dollars to spend on a record or tape, what would you buy? I'll give you several days to find out as much as you can about the musical group that made that record or tape. See what you can find out about the members of the group. What are their backgrounds, accomplishments, and hit records? Use magazine and newspaper articles or any other resource you can think of to help your research. Provide time for the students to share the information they've gathered.

Strengthening Language for Second-Language Learners

Activity 1

Objective
- to learn songs of different cultures

Materials
- Chart paper
- Markers

While the rest of the class listens, encourage groups of students to sing songs that are indigenous to their cultures. Help the students write the words to the songs on chart paper so that the rest of the class can sing along.

Activity 2

Objectives
- to listen to recordings of folk songs
- to recall words in folk songs

Materials
- Duplicating master
- Recordings of simple folk songs
- Record player or tape machine
- Marker
- Pencils

On the duplicating master, write the words to some simple folk songs. Distribute a copy of the master to each student. Have the students follow along as they listen to recordings of these songs. After the students have listened to the recordings several times, use a marker to block out specific words on each copy. Play the recordings again. Have the students listen carefully to the songs and try to fill in the missing words.

Reaching Across the Curriculum

Developing Creative Expression

Activity 1

Objective
- to write a description of an imaginary rock group

Materials
- Writing paper
- Pencils

Make up your own name for a rock group. Write a paragraph that describes the group and answers the following questions. What kind of music do they play? What instruments do they play? How old are they? How do they dress? How did they first get interested in music?

Activity 2

Objective
- to share musical recordings

Materials
- Records or tapes
- Record player or tape machine

Bring in a record or tape to share with the class. Be ready to tell the class something about the performing artists.

Activity 3

Objective
- to identify rock-and-roll songs

Materials
- Writing paper
- Pencils

If you were managing the group Igneous and the Metamorphics, which songs would you suggest they play? Make a list of rock-and-roll songs that you would like to hear them play.

Activity 4

Objective
- to see and hear actual musical instruments

Materials
- Musical instruments

Encourage students who are musically inclined to bring instruments to class to play and demonstrate. Seeing various instruments and hearing them played might spark interest among the students to learn more about instrument families, composers, history of music, etc. A unit of study could be developed around one of these musical topics.

Expanding Social Studies

Activity 1

Objective
- to conduct a survey of favorite musical groups

Materials
- Writing paper
- Pencils

Conduct a survey of the members of your family. Ask them who their favorite musical groups are. See if you can draw some conclusions from the information you have gathered. Share your information with the class. Describe the differences among the answers given. Determine if the age of the person answering makes a difference.

Activity 2

Objective
- to research favorite musical instruments

Materials
- Library sources
- Writing paper
- Pencils
- Drawing paper
- Crayons

Choose an instrument that a member of your favorite musical group plays. Find out as much as you can about the instrument. Write down your information. Draw a picture of the instrument. Have each student present her findings to the class.